D0934872

For Juan Antonio Montoya
1913–1982

THE WORLDS
OF P'OTSÚNÚ

THE WORLDS
OF P'OTSÚNÚ

Geronima Cruz Montoya
of San Juan Pueblo

Jeanne Shutes ▪ Jill Mellick

University of New Mexico Press

Albuquerque

Library of Congress Cataloging-in-Publication Data
Mellick, Jill.
The worlds of P'otsunu : Geronima Cruz Montoya of San Juan Pueblo/
Jill Mellick, Jeanne Shutes ; photography by Jeanne Shutes.—1st ed.
p. cm.
Includes index.
ISBN 0-8263-1643-3
1. P'otsunu, 1915- . 2. Tewa Indians—Biography. 3. Indian artists—
New Mexico—San Juan Pueblo—Biography.
I. Shutes, Jeanne, 1924- . II. Title.
E99.T35P686 1996
759.13—dc20
[B]   95-4412
                 CIP

TABLE OF CONTENTS

ACKNOWLEDGMENTS

We are grateful to P'otsúnú who gave us the gifts of her self, her trust, her time, and her records; and to family, friends, and colleagues for their support and assistance.

Christina Allen referred us to helpful ethnographic resources. Arlagene Bailey typed an early draft of the manuscript. Bruce Bernstein, Chief Curator and Assistant Director at the Laboratory of Anthropology of the Museum of Indian Arts and Culture, believed in the relevance and timeliness of our work and made contact with the University of New Mexico Press. Sarah Buttrey was a sensitive and skilled text editor. Bea Chauvenet provided us with written recollections of key figures in the early Santa Fe art world. Sandra P. Edelman gave us knowledgeable editorial assistance on the initial draft. John Fox transcribed later tapes. Elizabeth Gomperts worked with us in our early efforts to publish. Barbara Guth, our editor, encouraged us in our approach to this narrative and quietly and steadily navigated us through publication. Peter Hirose, Librarian at the Institute of Transpersonal Psychology and Laura Holt, Librarian at the Laboratory of Anthropology, Museum of Indian Arts and Culture, gave informative assistance. Etel Thea Kramer made an early painting by Jerry and the Dorothy Dunn Kramer collection of papers, in all its richness, available to us, the latter by donating it to the Archives of the

Laboratory of Anthropology. Dorothy Dunn Kramer (dec.) made private records available to us years ago, encouraged us, and sat and talked with us. Tsianina (Creek) and Hartman Lomawaima (Hopi) gave us constructive criticism and experienced, astute advice on narrative approaches and current ethnographic sources. Stanton Mellick gave us valuable criticism of the methodology sections. Robert Montoya (Sandia–San Juan), Jerry's oldest son, provided the genealogy, and offered constructive criticism of the manuscript. Susan Newton gave us extensive help with checking the accuracy of quotations, bibliographic cross-checking, reference-list preparation, and copyediting. Alfonso Ortiz gave valuable criticism of an early draft. Willow Powers, Archivist at the Laboratory of Anthropology, Museum of Indian Arts and Culture, assisted us with the Dorothy Dunn Kramer Collection. Edna Robertson at the Museum of New Mexico gave early research assistance. Barbara Stanislawski gave early archival assistance. Charlotte Zoe Walker published an earlier, excerpted version of this narrative in *Phoebe*, a State University of New York interdisciplinary journal. Peggy Weafer transcribed and typed our first draft.

Family members and friends of Jerry's and friends living in Santa Fe and in San Juan, Sandia, Cochiti, and Isleta Pueblos have also been most helpful speaking with us formally and informally and providing photographs: Liane Adams (dec.) (Santa Fe), Elidia Antoine (San Juan), Pauline Antoine (San Juan), Piedad Cruz Antoine (San Juan), Antonita (Queen) Arquero (San Juan), Sam Arquero (Cochiti), Sam Ballen (Santa Fe), Ethel Ballen (Santa Fe), Phyllis Crawford (dec.) (Santa Fe), Adelaide Cruz (dec.) (San Juan), Antonio García (dec.) (San Juan), Reycita Jirón (San Juan), Max Kramer (dec.), Margaret Mendez (Santa Fe), Domingo Montoya (dec.) (Sandia), Eugene Montoya (Sandia–San Juan), Juan Montoya (dec.) (Sandia), Mary Montoya (Sandia), Paul Montoya (Sandia–San Juan), members of the Oke Oweenge Crafts Cooperative (San Juan), Eva Oyenque (San Juan), Ramos Oyenque (dec.) (San Juan), Simonita Oyenque (San Juan), Mary Pease (Santa Fe), Janet Rosenwald (dec.) (Santa Fe), Carol Sandoval (San Juan), Ramoncita (Aunt Shine) Cruz Sandoval (San Juan), Letta Wofford (Santa Fe), and Arthur H. Wolf (Santa Fe).

Indians sense the creative forces still alive behind each created object.
They are aware that happiness, inspiration, and purpose in life
depend on an inner awakening, call it spiritual if you like.
Indians work with nature, not against it.
Indians try to understand the natural forces and work within them.

P'otsúnú

INTRODUCTION

Narrative Content, Context, and Structure

Geronima Cruz Montoya (Jerry) is a Pueblo Indian woman, Western educated, living in tricultural New Mexico. Her story is overlaid with many influences. Cultural threads interweave in the fabric of her experience. If it were told as she has lived it and as it has unfolded to us, her story would have no beginning, middle, or end; it does not define itself by linearity, chronology, or achievement.

If the structure of this narrative were truly one with its content and context, it would resemble Jerry's living room: a friendly blend of exquisite Indian paintings, Catholic religious items, books, photograph albums, magazines, minutes from meetings, pictures of grandchildren, plaques honoring her and Juan, comfortable places to be still or watch favorite programs, family members coming in and out unexpectedly, and the phone ringing with requests for Jerry's service on yet another board, her answers often given in an easy blend of Téwa and English. For us to organize Jerry's living room according to categories would seem as strange as our organizing this narrative. However, we did. There are beautiful objects hidden underneath the tables of Jerry's life and in pots of personal history. They would have been missed had we not decided to group some of the artifacts of memory.

Jerry belongs to an American Indian culture that, although heavily influenced by Western ideas of success, fundamentally seeks little, lives in the moment (not for the moment), and believes that its people, land, and mythology operate from a center, not along a trajectory. There is nowhere to go, and everything is done with love and integrity in order to maintain the balance of nature. Further, Jerry is a devout Catholic, and the values of selflessness, duty, and service run deep in her. As a self-described "traditional woman," too, she responds to what she perceives as the needs of her family and community more than to what she desires for herself.

All of these influences—her culture and its religion, her Catholicism, and her experience as a "traditional" Pueblo woman—have created a life lived in response to what the environment has seemed to offer or ask of her, a life lived in service, in understatement.

So achievement means little to Jerry. Her life does, of course, contain extraordinary achievements. She has secured these in the face of overwhelming social, cultural, and economic odds. She is a community leader in her own village of San Juan, in the wider Pueblo communities, and in the Southwestern multicultural community. She is an acclaimed artist and teacher whose vision and talent have been crucial in the development of and demand for American Indian art.

From a Western perspective, this is a good tale: plenty of events, obstacles, bad odds, successes. A tempting tale to tell—an heroic tale in the best of mythological traditions. However, to tell the tale using the content or the structure of a hero's myth is to misunderstand Jerry's experience and life as she has lived it and felt it. Instead, we seek ways by which Jerry's own experience and our subjective experiences of her might weave their own form. Since beginning this work in 1977, we have consciously refrained from structuring our narrative on historical, literary, artistic, or ethnographic precedents. And when we glimpsed new dimensions of Jerry's evolving life story, we set aside even our own precedents.

When we talked with Jerry about writing down her life and she—surprised at our interest—gave us permission, we gave her unconditional editorial rights: this was her story, to be told as much as possible as she saw it. The quality of the storytelling is therefore greatly muted from a Western viewpoint. Where you might expect emotional amplification, we give none; where you might expect detail, we give none; where you might expect crescendos of action or reaction, we give you a steady beat. At each of these points, we invite you to review and revise your own narrative expectations, rather than decide that something is missing. If you do this, you might briefly experience what Jerry has lived with all her life: the endless juxtaposition and interplay of worlds.

Many factors have determined the content, methodology, and structure of this narrative. Friendship is primary. The three of us all like and respect one another, and we, the authors, have great affection for, admiration for, and trust in Jerry. This research has been conducted—"has unfolded" is more accurate—in the context of friendship. As with many real-life situations, while the friendship came first and the research came later, each has challenged and nourished the other.

A second factor is Jerry's preferences. Jerry initiated none of the material in this book. Her statements are responses to questions we have put to her. It is not her way—or perhaps, not the conservative, Pueblo way—to volunteer much personal material unless asked—at least, not in speaking with Anglos. In informal conversations, Jerry has shared much; in formal conversations, she waits for questions and her answers are usually brief. The levels of details and events chronicled in this biography have been, therefore, subject to our capacity to ask questions that Jerry felt were appropriate and pertinent. Our questions have evolved out of material Jerry gave us, out of our own reading in anthropology, ethnology, biography, Southwestern art, and Southwestern history, and out of areas in which we have felt common grounds of experience with Jerry.

A third and even more important factor is the culturally determined activity of posing questions. Pueblo people do not generally seem to engage each other with questions, at least they do not when we hear them speaking among themselves or with non-Pueblo people in English. Furthermore, when Pueblo people speak English, they often seem emotionally reticent by Western standards. Since neither of us speaks Téwa, we have been limited to these observations. This creates a strong bias in content. While our intent is to tell this story as Jerry wishes it to be told, in fact we tell it as we believe Jerry wishes it to be told. Jerry has never told us, in nine revisions, that we need to include this or that. However, she has stated that things that are past and negative are better left unspoken and has often asked us to leave out some of her comments. While we have known, then, what Jerry wanted out of the narrative, we could never be sure what she wanted in; it has not been her way to speak about this. In Anglo fashion, at times we have asked her outright if she wanted us to add anything; Jerry has usually responded with thoughtful silence.

Because Jerry did not specify what she wanted included, we have tended to emphasize the content to which Jerry gave more time, energy, or emphasis and on which she provided more written material. These are Western criteria, based as they are on quantity. Other issues equally important to Jerry might well be unexpressed, unwritten, or executed in private—not intuited by us because of our cultural and personal biases. The depth and intensity that Jerry and her family have brought to a topic when we have raised it, however, does not necessarily correlate to the importance of that topic. It is curious to us, for example, that Jerry and her sisters remember none of the Pueblo stories they heard when they were children, given their parents' strong cultural affiliation and their own careful attention to all other aspects of Pueblo cultural life. It is curious to the sisters as well. Other situations or pieces of life history, such as her courtship with her husband, seem to have a different kind of relevance for Jerry than they would for us. That she says she never thinks about such a thing does not suggest that she accords the courtship less significance in her life, but simply that she never thinks about such a thing. Other events are remembered and recalled with some detail and emphasis. Many of these involve childhood, a major transitional moment such as a marriage or death, or events that have to do with bicultural situations such as school politics. We would not presume to theorize about why such events seem to evoke more discussion than others because, as we have pointed out, our presence as friends, narrative recorders, and interviewers influenced what was shared or garnered. The amount of narrative shared is difficult to distinguish from the amount of narrative remembered, although the distinction is relevant.

The unexpected factor of shared experiences among us has contributed to our focusing on certain subjects. All three of us went to schools that were founded on and inculcated such values as the work ethic, loyalty, and community service. All three of us taught in traditional, hierarchical teaching institutions and either created or maintained alternative creative arts curricula within them. We all left those institutions and sought more flexible ways of working, each becoming closely involved with adult education programs. We all have spent years in the arts, creating educational programs designed around what our adult students really want and need rather than what a curriculum board determines. We have all experienced different bicultural challenges and have had to find ways to make peace with their unresolvable aspects. We are all lifetime learners, having pursued education into adulthood and family life. As authors, we mention these commonalities not to show how alike we three are but to point out that shared interests and experiences influence how this story is told. We have been particularly curious about the unique ways in which Jerry has handled challenges similar to our own.

There are, of course, areas of our lives that share no common-alities. While we each carry a deep and private sense of the spiritual, our ways of expressing and sustaining this differ. We can only understand Jerry's participation in ceremonial life, for example, from the outside—from reading, from others' descriptions, and from our years of attending ceremonials as welcomed visitors. We can never know how it feels to Jerry to dance all day. To these areas, we have brought a circumspect curiosity.

Other influences on our narrative perspective are our own val-ues and histories. While they are too lengthy to include, it is worth noting that Jeanne grew up in New England and Jill in Australia, both environments in which discussion of one's personal life is not customary. Although we are each psychotherapists accustomed to listening to deeply personal material, we try not to intrude on oth-ers' privacy in our professional or personal lives; as does Jerry, we value privacy and share a natural and culturally reinforced reserve about discussing personal issues and showing feelings publicly. Other researchers might have asked Jerry more questions about her per-sonal life than we have, but perhaps Jerry has found us a little less annoying than some non-Indians because we have not.

Our professional experience also influences this narrative: we authors each bring background studies and professional work in the fields of English literature and Jungian psychology. These predispose us to appreciating the wealth of the symbolic realm. We find this perspective rich but have been cautious about creating symbolic connections that might satisfy our Western need for mythological coherence yet have little to do with Jerry's experience.

Another factor influencing the content of the narrative is the esoteric nature of Pueblo religion. We have no idea whether Jerry participates in closed ceremonies. This is neither ours to ask nor hers to tell. While Jerry describes herself as a layperson in her village, it is probably safe to assume that she has witnessed many events not open to outsiders. While some American Indian groups make their religious ideas and practices available to Westerners, Pueblo people do not. Even some hitherto public information has recently been withdrawn.

Too often Western storytellers in many disciplines impose hierarchical or predetermined forms on nonlinear and associative material. As we have said earlier, we neither can nor wish to treat content and structure as autonomous entities. Often different material within the same story demands a different form. The fluid narrative structures we have chosen to use represent the least intrusive way we have been able to devise to allow Jerry's material to freely breathe and move.

For recorded conversation, we use the standard first-person narrative form and do not include our questions. Jerry's comments stand well alone. However, given that Jerry does not volunteer information, the material should always be read with the assumption that questions preceded her commentaries. We do retain conversations between Jerry and Aunt Shine, when the evolution of the dialogue adds a feeling and tone that out-of-context quotations do not. The transcriptions also indicate the degree of consensus between Jerry and her sister on many issues.

We refer to cultural groups using the terms that they use for themselves. Jerry and her family and associates refer to themselves as "Indian" or "Pueblo." In using "American Indian," we thus stay with the term closest to Jerry's own. While "Native American" is preferred by many indigenous people, it is not used frequently by Pueblo people. In the same way, we do not refer to the Spanish-speaking people of New Mexico as "Hispanic," although this, too, is a preferred term now. The Spanish-speaking people of New Mexico whom we know in the villages refer to themselves as "Spanish." We also make use of "Anglo" because of its meaning to the Pueblo people: those people who are not Indian (that is, American Indian) and not Spanish. This covers a wider group than does the term "Western."

Although personally we have found it fascinating to read the unedited transcripts or, better still, to listen to the tapes with their texture of silences, we do minimally edit conversation. Our editing follows these principles:

Conversational fillers such as "um," "ah," "huh," and "yeah" are deleted.

Because much of our conversation was nonlinear and associative, we respect its spontaneity while still accommodating readers trained, like us, to expect rational topic development. A [*] indicates that material from different conversations is juxtaposed.

We delete none of Jerry's formal commentaries, although she has often removed material herself.

Every time Jerry read a draft, she rewrote many transcriptions, making them more formal, and often corrected the fluidity of tenses that characterizes her spoken English. She also asked that we, too, convert transcriptions into formal English. This is her material to be presented as she wishes, so we attempt to do this despite our preference for the original voice.

Our interweaving transcriptions from different interviews makes the final product sound like one long interview conducted in an eternal present—an inevitable and misleading outcome. These conversations and comments have been gathered over eighteen years. The first interviews were in 1977; the last, in 1994. As authors constantly growing and learning about ourselves and Jerry's world, our interests have evolved. Jerry's views, however, seem to remain constant. She seems just as at ease with her early comments as she is with her most recent. Her perspective seems based on her unfaltering values and on her feelings, which sustain themselves through collective tribal perceptions and Catholic perspectives. So, to read Jerry's comments as though they were all made from a fixed point in time and place is not to bypass interesting disparities and developments but to underemphasize her remarkable consistency and steadiness across the years.

Although the material seems chronological, we organize it by the worlds in which Jerry has moved. These worlds are differentiated by the predominant roles and activities of her life. Phase-specific activities are growing up, going to boarding school, learning to paint, teaching, starting the artist's cooperative, and retiring. Cyclical activities are her family, religious, and ceremonial lives and her painting. Within each world we offer a series of narrative images, often built around Jerry's own narration and titled, where possible, with a quote from or about Jerry. Sometimes, we build them around a particular activity or event, which we report in the third person.

Each of Jerry's worlds is also differentiated by a set of mores and expectations, even within one cultural framework. The world of childhood in San Juan Pueblo, far from Western interference, had vastly different mores from the world of the federal boarding school to which Jerry was sent in fifth grade; the world of teaching had very different expectations of Jerry from those of the ceremonial cycle in San Juan and Sandia Pueblos.

The consciousness and values she has brought to each of these worlds are what weave them together; otherwise, their very differences might have sundered her spirit.

We attempt to include just enough context to enable appreciation of the skills, fortitude, creativity, and adaptability Jerry brings to each and some feeling for the natural forces and mores of the worlds in which Jerry has moved and moves. Too much context might predetermine a reader's response to the narrative. We also attempt to rein in our theorizing about Jerry's actions, responses, or feelings. Still, some understanding of the political, educational, assimilative, and emotional pressures on the children who were sent to federal boarding schools, for example, helps us—and we hope others—to appreciate what was universal among the students and what was unique to Jerry's experience. Some understanding of the virulent battles for and against "traditional art" helps us appreciate the seemingly contradictory blend of Jerry's unshakable fidelity to traditional artistic philosophy, her democratic approach to teaching, and personal artistic flexibility.

This is a narrative by and about a woman who happens to be an artist as well as many other things. We do not intend this to be the biography of an artist who happens to have lived a life. We all three consider her paintings to be part of a wider context. Jerry paints because she enjoys painting, and she likes her paintings to illustrate her inner and outer life as a Pueblo woman. She is not interested in using her life story or formal art theory to analyze or interpret her painting; we, too, have reined in these musings.

Our primary oral sources are informal conversations and structured interviews with Jerry and her extensive family. We have documented in several ways: detailed written summaries, tapes, transcriptions, and photographs. Jeanne held meetings in the summers of 1977 and 1978 with Jerry; her husband, Juan; and her sisters Piedad, Aunt Shine, and Reycita. These she recorded by hand. Later meetings took place with both of us; Jill taped and transcribed these. From 1971 through 1994 Jeanne kept visual records, taking hundreds of slides of family events, ceremonials, significant places, and family paintings and crafts. Jeanne first spoke with Dorothy Dunn in 1971, and we both visited Dunn in 1978. Jill coincidentally met Dunn once again when she was terminally ill and living at a facility where Jill was the consulting psychologist.

Primary written sources include Jerry's records, to which she has given us access. Other family records, written and visual, have been loaned to us. Dorothy Dunn also gave us copies of her personal correspondence with Jerry.

Our other primary sources are treasured experiences of being included in Montoya and Cruz family events, such as family picnics in Jerry's backyard, baptisms, breakfasts and coffee times with each of the sisters and other relatives, letters and phone calls, and the opportunity to host Jerry and other family members in Palo Alto. We have watched Jerry and other family members dance in ceremonials and joined them at their homes on ceremonial days.

Co-authorship is an exercise in conscious mutuality and sensitive division of labor. We have played complementary roles in writing this book. Jeanne made and consolidated our connections with Jerry's family and did the initial interviewing, genealogical work, and historical research over the first three years. Jill then joined the project and formally interviewed Jeanne about her research; those transcripts became the first draft. Both have participated in and taped, transcribed, and taken notes on fifteen years of subsequent conversations and research with Jerry and her family. Jill, in consultation with Jeanne, has done all subsequent writing and editing, providing, in particular, the reflections on Jerry's worlds, the studio chapter, and this introduction.

Jeanne has also built the photographic documentary of Jerry, her paintings, and her family over twenty years by taking hundreds of slides, copies of which she has given to Jerry; all nonarchival photography in the book is Jeanne's. In all cases the wishes of the Pueblo were respected regarding photography. Permission was always obtained in advance to photograph, and the proper permits were purchased from the kiva groups performing.

The final influence on this narrative is what is not made visible. What is not spoken is a vital element in this story, as strong as any other. The narrative resembles the forms, lines, and color blocks of Jerry's paintings. The silence resembles the large unpainted spaces that Jerry allows. In Western art, this unpainted area is termed "negative" space; in Eastern art, it is seen as the numinous, eternal present about to reveal itself. This latter view is more akin to our experience of Jerry's narration of her life. The experiences she describes are like the figures and forms she paints: she distills them into formal essences, usually without location or date, without shadow or detail, but suspended in a numinous moment. The experiences that Jerry does not describe, and we do not know, belong to that silent, eternal space.

1
AT THE CENTER
OF THE EARTH
Childhood in San Juan

Gathering Family Memories

Geronima (Jerry) Cruz Montoya lives the spirit of her mother and father every time she travels to San Juan for administrative, ceremonial, or familial reasons, every time she walks by the old adobe house on the plaza where she grew up, every time she passes the family's summer house still sheltered by cottonwood trees, every time she goes to Mass or participates in a ceremonial dance. For Jerry and her four sisters, their parents, Pablo Cruz and Crucita Trujillo, have been the most important influences on their individually remarkable lives. This is not unusual. However, the extent to which each of these five women has consciously lived this experience is unusual.

The sisters' spoken memories about their early childhood are not numerous. For Jerry, her childhood experience of Pueblo life, although severed early because of governmental schooling requirements, run so deep in her that it does not require description. It just is—in the present—within her and alive, not an artifact to be turned over in the mind like a pottery shard in the hand.

We gathered these childhood images during and after many visits to San Juan Pueblo from 1976 to 1994. Different family members, including the sisters, have shown us, at our request, the village

The entrance to San Juan Pueblo, as seen from the Day School, 1972. The old mercantile store is on the right.

places of ongoing importance in their lives, family heirlooms, and treasured family photographs and news clippings. The sisters and their children have spoken with us formally and informally over the years about their childhood experiences.

San Juan Pueblo

Located on the winding Rio Grande and among the four mountains that are the spiritual origins of the ancestors, San Juan Pueblo is one of eight Pueblo Indian villages north of the New Mexico capital of Santa Fe.

The first Western report of the village dates back to 1541 when one of Coronado's captains reported finding two villages, Yunque Yunque and O'ke, in the area. These villages predated the Conquistadores by at least two hundred years. In 1598, Don Juan de Oñate located his own settlement at Yunque Yunque, renamed it San Gabriel, and declared it the first capital of North Mexico, which then included what is now Colorado, Arizona, New Mexico, and parts of Texas. O'ke was renamed San Juan de los Caballeros.

After the Spaniards settled San Gabriel, the villagers gradually moved east to San Juan. At first they had welcomed the Spaniards, but these farmers and traders eventually tired of their guests' attraction to gold and slaves, and so the Spaniards moved their capital to La Villa Real de Santa Fé in 1605.

In 1680, Popé, a San Juan medicine man who had been attempting to defend Indians accused of witchcraft, led the Pueblos in a successful rebellion. For a brief time after the rebellion, San Juan became the Pueblo capital of the area, which remained independent until reconquered by the Spaniards in 1695.

Today, the Téwa-speaking village with its 2,300 inhabitants has an architectural mix that echoes its history. It has two rectangular kivas, or ceremonial/social meeting chambers. St. John the Baptist Catholic Church and the Chapel of Our Lady of Lourdes are both imitation French Gothic. A modern pueblo-style building houses the Oke Oweenge Crafts Cooperative. Traditional adobe houses border the three plazas. Farther away from the center of the village lie unadorned federal government–issue houses, often painted colors like turquoise, unexpected to the Western eye. In the shade of their open verandas, young children play and hardy village dogs of indeterminate breed sleep the hours away or bark at pickups stirring dust. Even farther from the village and secreted by tall grasses lie the low adobe ruins of Yunque O'winge, the village's original center. The remains of an adobe wall mark the original church of San Gabriel, claimed to be the oldest building erected by Europeans in North America.

Some men still farm their land, growing corn and other crops; some work at nearby Los Alamos Laboratories. Some women care for children or extended family at home while some work with their crafts—art, pottery, weaving, embroidery—or work outside of the village in Santa Fe or Española. It is not an economically rich village.

The Cruz Family Home

At the turn of the century, Pablo Cruz and Crucita Trujillo's first family home in San Juan was a two-roomed adobe house bordering the main plaza, into which they moved in 1901. Life revolved

(ABOVE) *The two-room adobe house on the south plaza of San Juan Pueblo. Owned by Uncle Romaldo, the cacique, it was Jerry's birthplace and housed the family until 1935.* (BELOW) *The entrance to the summer house by the acequia madre.*

around the center of the village, and the center of the village was the main plaza. For the Cruz family, their tiny house was located at the center of their physical and spiritual world. At one time, the house was home to eight family members. Today, still belonging to the Cruz family, its windows are boarded up and its inhabitants dispersed to other houses in the pueblo and other towns.

In 1935, the Cruz family moved from their small house to the cooler "summer house," a cottonwood-shaded adobe beside the acequia, the irrigation ditch that provides water for the fields. Originally, the house belonged to Reycita, a first cousin who was adopted into the family as a daughter. Not wanting the house for herself, she gave it to the family, who then gave her other land in exchange. Wanting it shared equally, Pablo and Crucita declared, "The house belongs to all the family." When they decided to live there all year long, they were the only family living outside the actual "pueblo," the common-wall units built around the plaza.

Although only a few minutes away, the summer house at first seemed to the family to be far from the center of the world, the main plaza, where their ancestors had danced in ceremonials for hundreds of years and later walked across to the church for baptisms, First Communions, marriages, and burials. The house lies a short walk east along a soft dust road toward the acequia.

Over the decades, the house has absorbed subtle changes: new bread-baking hornos between the house and the acequia, electricity. Much has not changed: the view of cottonwood trees from the low kitchen window in front of the sink where thousands of dishes from family and village feasts have been washed; the Navajo rugs on the floors; the family-made pottery on the mantelpiece; the large dining table.

Except for her few years at the Santa Fe Indian School, Adelaide (Oyegi), the oldest of the five Cruz sisters, lived in the house until her death in 1979. Piedad (Pie), the next sister, after going away to boarding school, marrying, and living in Santa Fe as a young widow, returned and has lived with her daughter Pauline close by the family house much of her life. Her other daughter, Elidia, also lives nearby with her own family. The three youngest Cruz sisters, Jerry (Geronima), Aunt Shine (Ramoncita), and Reycita (Rey), married and moved away to Santa Fe and Isleta Pueblo.

Over the sixty-odd years since they completed their high school educations, however, Jerry and Aunt Shine have returned, usually weekly, to the village: to show off new babies to their parents, care for their ailing parents, visit Adelaide, volunteer weekly at the crafts cooperative, and sing in the Téwa choir. Whenever possible, each sister and her family members also return to the pueblo for ceremonial days and, on Easter, Thanksgiving, and Christmas, to dance or to bake bread and cook food for their large extended family, sometimes cooking for over two hundred guests on San Juan Feast Day.

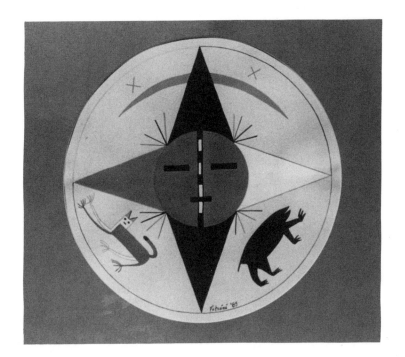

(OPPOSITE) *Juan Pablo and Crucita Trujillo Cruz on a picnic with the family in the Pecos Wilderness, 1920s. Family archives.* (ABOVE) *"Shield Design and Four Directions." Shiva casein by P'otsúnú, 1981.*

The Birth, Naming, and Baptism of Geronima

In 1915, trips to Santa Fe were rare, even for those living close; wagon journeys were costly, long, and arduous. Rarely was it necessary to be more than a day's round-trip from the pueblo. Pablo Cruz, out tending his corn and chile on the clear September afternoon when his daughter Geronima was born, would have been able to see his whole world and all four of the mountains sacred to his people: to the north, Canjilon Peak; to the east, Truchas Peak in the Sangre de Cristo spur of the Rockies; to the south, Sandia Crest; and to the west, Chicoma (Tsikumu) Mountain. He would have felt at the center of the world.

In the house on the plaza, two midwives helped Crucita with the birth of her fifth child. (Her first, a son, and her fourth, a daugh-

(LEFT) *"Presentation to the Sun." Shiva casein by P'otsúnú, 1978. The midwives are responsible for giving a Pueblo child her names. Here they take the new baby to greet the sun.* (RIGHT) *"Taking Lunch." Shiva casein by P'otsúnú, 1982.*

ter, both died shortly after birth, as would her sixth child.) Her older daughters—Adelaide, now twelve, and Piedad, nine—were away from the house. Later, their fourth daughter, Ramoncita, would be born, and Crucita's niece, Reycita, would be welcomed as the fifth.

"I was born September 23 according to the baptismal certificate and church records, but my father said it was September 22, so that's the date I go by," says Jerry. At dawn, four days after the birth, Crucita and the two midwives took the infant out to greet the sun, rising quickly above the thirteen-thousand-foot Truchas Peak. For the San Juan people, "The East is the most important direction in daily life because of its identification with the sun, which is believed to be the fertilizing agent in nature" (Oregon Address, 1973).

According to Jerry's memory of her mother's story, each of the midwives gave her a name in Téwa: one called her "Phóyé Póvi" (Autumn Flower); the other called her "P'otsúnú" (Pink Shell). The archival records held at the village church indicate that she was baptized on October 3 by Father Simón Alverhue. There she was given the additional Spanish name "María Gerónima," a name she says was suggested by her San Juan godparents, José Ignacio Torres and Presentación Chávez. As a child, Jerry was known as "Phóyé Póvi"; later, she would use "P'otsúnú" as her public name as a painter. When she went away to school she was nicknamed

"Jerry," and "Jerry," being the easiest to pronounce, became the name she has used most frequently through her life.

Táa: "I Was Close to My Dad."

Pablo Cruz was known as a deeply spiritual man and as a magnificent farmer. He farmed on nine fields near Alcalde. Such was the quality of Pablo Cruz's chile crop that neighbors from San Juan and nearby villages tried to get seeds from Pablo's chile for their own land. He worked long days for the quality of his crops, and the whole family worked with him. As children, all five sisters rose early to help Táa (Father) with the farming.

We got up at dawn to help with planting corn and chile or cutting wheat and hauling alfalfa. I was close to my dad. I guess because I was always working with him or bringing him his lunch and eating with him.

We took the noon meals out to Father and, maybe midmorning and afternoon, we took out a refreshment. We'd stay until he ate and when he was through, we'd leave. We usually took him stew, coffee, and hot tortillas. We had a basket with bread and a dish and a cup and sugar.

We went out more than he came in. We hardly saw him in the summer. If we went out with him to the fields, then we'd come in for lunch, but if we were going to Alcalde, three miles north of San Juan, we'd take lunch. We would eat lunch sitting on the back of the wagon.

That particular field is mine now but wasn't planted for a long time after Father died. Now the farmers' cooperative, of which I'm a member, is planting there again.

We had to cut wheat with a sickle. When you looked down the wheat fields, you just wanted to cry! There was so much to cut! When we had others help, we went home to cook for them. Relatives helped and never expected pay.

I also went out with my father to gather wood in the hills east of the pueblo and help him load. Wood was used for heating and cooking on the wood stove.

We would also take feed and water to the chickens, often treading along in the snow.

When Pablo brought loads of chile and corn around the trade circuit of small villages north of San Juan, Jerry would go with him.

We used to travel together in the wagon to sell or trade. We'd have breakfast on the other side of Black Mesa near the Ojo Caliente River and get to Ojo Caliente by noon. We'd have corn and sacks of chile, apples, plums, and pottery. We sold a bucket of chile for twenty-five cents. Now you pay two dollars to five dollars a bucket.

We stayed overnight with the Jaramillo family in Ojo Caliente and the next day went on to La Madera. By evening, we'd get to La Madera and we'd stay overnight. We always stayed overnight with Spanish friends. We slept in their home. They gave us breakfast of the most delicious hot tortillas and boiled milk with atole and chile. Those people were very kind and unselfish and shared what they had.

From La Madera, we went to Vallecitos and stayed with the De Vargas family, and the next day we went to Cañones and back to Vallecitos where we stayed another night. The next day we headed for home. Sometimes we slept in the wagon. Dad had hay on the wagon floor and we would put our blankets over that.

Father was very good to all of his work horses so he had food for them, too. One of Dad's horses was called Cantanu, named after the man he bought the horse from. The folks would go up to Taos for San Gerónimo's fiesta and stay there to trade. After the feast, they returned to San Juan. On one occasion, when they were returning to San Juan, Cantanu dropped dead—right at the turnoff to San Juan! The good horse had brought them home safe. That shows how faithful the horse was! Mother and Father felt so bad, they walked home all the way from the branch-off to the house. We went up there and tried to give Father a ride home but Father said "No." We buried the horse near the road, right there, where it died.

When my parents went to the mountains to pick piñon nuts, I have been told that my sister, Pie, would take care of me for days. That was another way of making their livelihood because they sold the piñon nuts.

It was hard. We were poor and we didn't have any money to go gallivanting around. We were lucky if we had a nickel! But we didn't starve and we were happy. We had vegetables all the time from the farm, and Mother had her pottery to bring in a little money. We also had chickens, pigs, and cows, so we had milk, eggs, chicken, beef, and pork.

Equally important and constant for Pablo was his ceremonial and religious life. Pablo was active in Indian religious activities and danced in the ceremonials. "He danced Basket Dance, Turtle Dance, and Butterfly Dance. He participated in the dances and knew the songs and sang them. He liked to hold the kids on his lap and sing to them."

Pablo was also a devoted Catholic:

Father was sacristan at the pueblo church for over twenty-seven years. First he served for Fathers Simón and Camilio. When they died, he served twenty-seven years for Father Pajot. He served Mass all those years, and every day, at six in the morning, at noon, and at six in the evening, he rang the bell for the Angelus. When he was out in the fields, we would ring the bell for him. He knew all of the Church Latin and could pray in Latin and Spanish, so he taught Latin to some of the younger men so that they could serve Mass. His prayer books are in Spanish and Latin, which he read daily. When he became blind, he couldn't serve any more.

Pauline, Piedad's older daughter, adds: "Our grandfather was a very devout Christian who raised us in the old ways. He taught us to respect each other and our family. That's why we are all so close to each other."

Yíyá: Mother and Potter

Crucita was a craftswoman: she was a fine cook, expert sewer, and renowned potter. "She was a good cook. She was very particular. She would rather do it herself than have us do it. So that is why we didn't learn much!" For breakfast, Crucita usually fixed her husband and daughters *sa'kewe*, a mush made with water and meal from

Jerry's mother, Crucita, and older sister Adelaide, baking bread in the horno behind the summer house for the feast day of St. John the Baptist, 1930s or 1940s. Family archives.

the special blue corn grown in the village. "We still eat it for breakfast. But we rarely drank milk. We like milk but it doesn't like us. The doctor told me that we Indian people just can't digest lactose."

Yíyá (Mother) also taught the girls how to bake many kinds of bread—a central part of village family and ceremonial life. Behind the family home were two hornos: the smaller adobe oven was used for roasting chile and the larger for baking bread. Years later, Jerry would write about what she had learned from Yíyá about bread:

> What I have been able to find out about the Pueblo bread is that the Spanish and the Franciscan missionaries taught the Pueblo Indians how to make the bread and bake it in the beehive-shaped oven. Before the time of Columbus and the Spaniards, the Indians used corn meal for their bread. When the Spanish and missionaries came to the Southwest, they brought wheat to the Pueblos. . . .
>
> Before the time of commercial yeast, the women saved fermented

dough to start a new bread but that is no longer done. Today they use commercial yeast entirely to make bread.

The unusual shape does not have any special significance. Each type, however, does have a special name. The three-finger type is called *mandi*, which means *hand*. The Parker House type is called *pân*. There is another type, *siki'nä*, that is round with pinched edges with small pieces on top called *flowers*. This type of bread is called *ką̧ą wó-i*, meaning mixed with lard. This type of bread is made for special occasions, such as ceremonials, dances, weddings, and other feasts where baskets of foods are given away. In order to make the baskets of food attractive, they make these special decorative breads to include with other foods.

Other types of bread baked in the outdoor ovens are two kinds of pies, *pahtây* and *sito'i*; cookies, *puú-tsi*; [and] sweet-bread, *ap'o wóei*. Molasses is used in this type of bread.

In some of the pueblos, a smaller type of bread is made with a hole through the middle. The hole is just big enough for yucca fiber to go through on which the bread is strung and can be carried. It is used in certain dances.

The Pueblo bread is made for any big gathering such as fiestas, weddings, and dances. A whole day is set aside ordinarily for baking because it takes anywhere from a half day to three quarters of a day depending on the amount and occasion. But for weddings and funerals the relatives get together and help with the baking. They bake a whole day and sometimes use more than one oven. (Unpublished article)

Crucita also taught her daughters how to sew, Pueblo-style. There were no sewing machines used in the Cruz family—nor were scissors used for traditional clothing. All "cutting" and sewing was done by hand. The sisters learned how to tear the cotton into strips. Some would be used to make the yoke and gathered bodice on the loose dresses; other pieces would be finely pleated to decorate high collars and long, close-fitting cuffs. Jerry was the least adept of the sisters at sewing. As they grew older, Aunt Shine and Piedad became prizewinning sewers, embroiderers, and weavers. Aunt Shine recalls:

My mother was an expert at sewing. Instead of cutting, she would just tear the pieces for the collar and the sleeves of the traditional San Juan dresses that she made. When I come across old rags, I still see her sewing. She taught me how to do the Téwa dresses. That's where I learned.

If she had to do something special she would do it herself instead of asking us but I guess she was afraid we were not going to do it right. So she did it herself.

While Yíyá made their special ceremonial and traditional dresses, everyday, non-Indian dresses were mainly bought. According to Aunt Shine:

We wore the regular clothing. I know we used to order from the catalogue. That I remember. Montgomery [Ward], I think. [*] We used to order from the catalogues because we didn't have a way of coming to town. Or sometimes we bought fabric at the General Store. I think Mother did make us some regular clothes.

According to Adelaide, Yíyá made Jerry a new dress for Christmas when Jerry was quite young, but Yíyá told her that she couldn't wear it until it was time for dancing. Jerry was dying to wear it. One day, she went over to the kiva where she saw the dancers practicing for Christmas, rushed home to Yíyá, and said, "Why not now? They're dancing!"

Clothes for eight family members meant lots of laundry:

I used to hate it when Pie and Adelaide had to wash clothes because I had to fill three tubs! And we had to warm the water and then wash on the wash board. First wash and then two rinses.

There was a pump right there. [*] It's no longer there now. They knocked that out since they put in the water and sewer system. They knocked the pump out.

We used the iron that you heat on the top of the stove to do the ironing. No electric irons. [*] We were all responsible for the ironing. [*] Saturday, I think, was when we did the ironing.

If Pablo was well-known and respected for his farming, Yíyá was equally well-known and respected for her pottery, which she crafted in the traditional coil method. The slip, made from red clay, gave the pottery its distinctive San Juan glaze. "She, too, was an artist," says Jerry. According to Aunt Shine:

> Usually she made pottery. And then she also helped in the fields. [*] I think when she was making pottery she didn't go into the fields. But there were certain days that she made her pottery. But, you know, it seemed that when we woke up in the morning she was already sitting there making pots. You could just hear her pounding on her clay to get all the air out.

And on those pottery days, the girls would fix their own corn mush and breakfast while she was working.

Piedad remembers that, when she and Adelaide were teenagers, they would help Yíyá finish her pots by carefully bundling the dried pottery in baskets and carrying them down behind the summer house to fire near the chicken coop. There they would build the mound of dry cow dung and bake the pottery, which would turn either red or black depending on how they covered it with dung. Jerry remembers being allowed to help Crucita polish a pot to its high, smooth glaze using her mother's precious polishing stone, a family legacy. She also remembers how, many years later, her husband would help Crucita with her pottery making: "After Juan and I were married, Juan would take her to the clay pits. People from the pueblo wanted to dig their clay. My father would get the cow dung for firing and the pumice to mix in the clay. We call [the pumice] 'shu̧'yä̧.'"

When the pots were fired and finally polished, Jerry and Aunt Shine would sell them by the side of the highway.

> Ramoncita and I would sell in a shed covered with cottonwood branches, beside the highway. Three or four of us girls from the pueblo would take a lunch and stay all day. A large pot would sell for fifteen dollars, a bowl for three dollars, and a small one for fifty cents. If we made twenty or twenty-five dollars, we felt really good and practically ran home with our bundles and earnings.

One magnificent wedding olla still in the family shows a price of six dollars.

While prices were low, even for the value of the dollar then, the quality of Crucita's pottery was high. As the *Albuquerque Journal* of October 19, 1941, reported:

> Mrs. Crucita T. Cruz, San Juan Pueblo, was awarded a prize of $50 Saturday for her pottery exhibit in the Syracuse, New York, Museum of Fine Arts Tenth Annual Ceramic Exposition. . . .
>
> Mrs. Cruz's award was for a decorated plate. Crucita Cruz's exhibits were sent by the Pueblo Indian Arts and Crafts . . . organization sponsored by the United Pueblos Agency [Bureau of Indian Affairs (BIA)] to encourage quality work. . . .
>
> Mrs. Cruz won first and second prize in the pottery division of the Gallup Intertribal Ceremonial last August, 1941.

The Syracuse exposition included pottery and sculpture exhibits from 15 South and Central American countries as well as those from 500 North American artists. From the latter group, the judges selected 480 pieces, the work of 200 artists.

Jerry remembers her mother receiving many other "firsts and seconds" at the Gallup event and at the Santa Fe Fiesta exhibit. For a time, Crucita had a contract with a pottery shop in Santa Fe, and she continued to make pottery almost until her death in 1969. Her potting ability passed on, particularly to Aunt Shine.

As well as being a skilled potter, Crucita was a fine ceremonial dancer. According to Aunt Shine:

> Long ago—they used to ask the women to dance. When they had Cloud Dance or Buffalo Dance, they went and asked the women to take part. It was an honor. And they did it in a different way: they talked to you first. Then, they selected older people. But now all of that is gone. The ladies volunteer now. The ladies volunteer, especially for the cloud dance.
>
> [*] My mother was involved a lot of times. [*] She was chosen to dance.

Crucita passed on her dancing to her daughters too; Jerry and Aunt Shine still love to attend dances and dance. Crucita's looks, however, according to Jerry, were passed on to Piedad:

> Pie resembles Mother a lot. When Pie dresses Indian, she looks just like Mother walking around. Mother had wonderful sight. She could see clear across from here who was coming and who was going. Of course, she lost her hearing in the last years. They say Pie and I look a lot alike but we don't see it.

Ceremonial and Sacrament

Like many Pueblo families, the Cruz household sustained their traditional religion, participating in the ceremonial duties. While the daughters learned early from Crucita how to dance, they had to wait longer to learn about Pueblo religious life. Asked about who did the passing on of Indian lore to them, Aunt Shine reflects:

> I guess Mother did more. Father didn't tell us much about our Indian way. They said, "In time, you learn—just don't ask questions." We had to wait and we felt "when the time is right, then they will tell us"—which they did.

They had to wait, apparently, until they were much older before they were told.

Stories, however, were told freely on winter evenings. To her regret, Jerry does not remember the special myths or stories she heard as a child. "I don't remember any of the stories." Aunt Shine also remembers only hearing the stories:

> I think long ago—when we were growing up, you know—we used to visit relatives in the winter and we took turns—they took turns— telling stories. I was just telling them lately, I said, "Gosh it is too bad we didn't have a tape recorder at the time. We could have taped them and we would have all that." Now I can't remember any of the stories.

While they might not now recall exactly what they heard during their winter evenings with relatives, the sisters are aware of the importance of oral history. As Aunt Shine says:

> It is [important]! We were small. It was boring for us when the elders were telling the stories. One would tell one story and then another one would tell another story. That is how we spent our winters: visiting relatives, eating piñon, fresh corn, coffee. We did! Now, we don't even visit any more. We are so busy at home. We are watching the tube. .

The family also had the honor of sharing their small house on the plaza with Pablo's uncle, Romaldo Cruz, who was one of the pueblo's two hereditary caciques, or indigenous religious leaders.

> Uncle Romaldo lived with us until his death. His Indian name was Fir or Douglas Fir—Tsay K'ąą. Curtis [the nineteenth-century photographer] took a picture of him.
>
> Another great-uncle of ours wove and embroidered a manta himself. He was a fine weaver. Mother gave this manta to her half-brother for his bride. [*] Both San Juan caciques are dead now and there is no one to replace them.

In addition to introducing their five daughters early to the customs and duties of Pueblo religious life, Crucita and Pablo drew them into the practices and beliefs of the Catholic Church. The parents had each of their daughters baptized; each also received First Communion.

When the Cruz family celebrated Christmas, their Spanish friends from the northern villages would come down to San Juan to attend Mass and see the Matachine dances—reenactments of an ancient Spanish-Moorish legend, still performed in many Pueblo and Spanish villages at different times of the year but always on Christmas Eve and Christmas day in San Juan. "One time at Christmas when all the Spanish people came to see the dances, on Christmas Eve, they slept on a bed in our living room and we slept under the table in the kitchen." Spanish people respected

(LEFT) *Jerry's uncle Romaldo Cruz, cacique of the winter moiety, San Juan Pueblo, early 1930s. Family archives.* (RIGHT) *Jerry, after taking her First Communion at age eight in front of St. John the Baptist Catholic Church, San Juan Pueblo, 1923. Family archives.*

the Pueblo religious practices in other ways, especially believing in the efficacy of certain Pueblo pilgrimages.

Crucita and Pablo's teachings and the teachings of the church have been mainstays of each sister's life ever since. The sisters sang for years in the church choir under the direction of Antonio García, musician and member of the pueblo, and over sixty years later they still sing in the church and attend Mass with unvarying regularity.

I guess I'm just an old traditionalist and prefer Gregorian chants to the present-day music. I think Latin sounds better. It's more universal than the Mass in English. There was a time when you could go to any Catholic church for Mass and know just what to expect, but now each is different.

The sisters' active involvement in the Catholic Church has remained steady over the years, through joys and sorrows that might have shredded the fabric of lesser faiths. The sisters have also brought their talents to the service of the church in many ways. Although preferring the traditional music, Jerry and two other choir members in recent years composed music for a special Téwa Mass. Jerry explains that these melodies are "naturally Pueblo but not copies of Pueblo chants." While she reads music and plays the piano, she composed the music in her head and then put it on tape, helped by one of her favorite nuns, Sister Ann Rozalia Szabo, O.P., who led the choir after Tony García.

As a prizewinning embroiderer, Aunt Shine uses her own talents in the service of the church. "I could always think of designs. I used to make designs for my mother's pottery. Designs in embroidery came the same way to me," she says. She embroidered vestments for Father Edmund Sevilla, the first Southwestern Indian to be ordained a priest, and for former New Mexico archbishop Robert Sánchez. And the sisters are all active in the national movement dedicated to the canonization of Tekakwitha, an Indian woman.

Jerry has deep, active connections with both Pueblo Indian and Roman Catholic beliefs and practices. While the demands on her time and energies from this dual commitment have been high, the demands on her spirit have not been: "There is no conflict for me. Both Indian and Catholic religions offer faith, hope, serenity." Her sister Reycita's comments are uncannily similar: "One complements the other. There is no conflict that I can see. Both believe in one supreme being."

"They Showed Their Love in . . . a Very Quiet Way."

All the sisters are agreed and unqualified in their positive views about their parents and the Pueblo values their parents instilled. They were strongly influenced by these values of sharing, undemonstrative love, hard work, and kindness. According to Jerry and Aunt Shine, Yíyá was the one who managed discipline in the household. As Aunt Shine recalls: "She was very strict. She did all the discipline.

My father didn't. [*] When she would get cross with us, she would tell us."

Yíyá, like any mother of five bright daughters, was challenged daily. Reycita remembers a San Juan Feast Day (June 24) when she was a young child.

One Feast Day, I remember swinging on the cupboard at home and I toppled it over just as many Santa Clara people came to visit and eat with us. All the dishes got broken and mixed up with the sugar and syrup that had been in the cupboard, and Mother scolded me a lot. She made me clean it all up and take out the trash. I felt terrible about it.

Yíyá's granddaughter Pauline remembers: "My grandmother had a deep voice and I was a little afraid of her—but my grandfather always took my side."

Asked if they were "good" children, Aunt Shine replies with light vehemence:

We had to be! We had to be! We had to be! I remember one time when we moved to where the old house is now. They used to have dances in the kiva. My friends came to the house so that we could go to the dance at the kiva and she wouldn't let me go. And I would ask my father and he said "No, she told you 'no,' so you stay home." So I had to stay home and my friends had to go without me. That time—I remember that part because my friends came to pick me up at the house and [they] didn't let me go. I felt so bad and I used to wish we were living in the pueblo [plaza area]—you know, so I could attend things like that.

Asked about what values she believes her parents gave her that have lasted her through her life, Jerry responds:

To be honest and respect family. They showed their love in a different way—a very quiet way. Not hugging. They never used harsh words. They were kind and understanding.
[*] Mother and Father never did anything to hurt anybody. If you

took something away from Father, he wasn't going to fight back. The love is there in our family but we don't express it openly. To me love is sacred and personal and you just don't go around showing it everywhere even though you feel it. We're very close as a family. Sometimes I wonder if we're too close. We maybe should go out and discover the world instead of staying protected. Many of the Indian youths stick around home and then get into trouble. Maybe if we weren't so close, they would get out and take care of themselves.

[*] Somehow we [family] all try to amount to something, be somebody, earn our own living and not be dependent on anybody. Yet we're close. The family ties are there. We always felt that our parents gave everything for us so that we would have good lives and so we had to do for them, too. Our parents taught us to be honest, respectful, kind, and helpful—to learn to share and love.

Aunt Shine adds:

And sharing—I know one time I was at the Day School—that one day my dad was planting corn and I had to go help him and I cried because I couldn't go to school and because I had to go help him drop corn in the field. While he was plowing, I had to drop the corn behind him. Five or six kernels. Every three feet or so. That part I remember.

[*] And then when I came home, we all had our chores. He used to chop wood and my job was to take all the wood that he chopped in for the night—to keep the house warm and to cook. And I also had to go and get water.

While chores were assigned, certain days to do them were not. As Jerry says, "We just lived from one day to the next." Adelaide remembered that the sisters spent much of their time helping Yíyá with household tasks. In a large Pueblo family, even small children always had chores to do—roasting chile, baking bread, gathering wood, getting water from the spring, washing the dishes with the water heated on the wood stove. Every morning before breakfast, the sisters would help Yíyá by walking south past the priest's house and down by the willow to the spring to get water. Jerry remembers:

(TOP LEFT) *"Washing Hair." Shiva casein by P'otsúnú, 1983. Jerry and her sisters washed their hair this way when they were growing up in the pueblo.* (BOTTOM LEFT) *"Getting Water at the Spring." Shiva casein by P'otsúnú, 1975.* (RIGHT) *"Mother and Children." Shiva casein by P'otsúnú, 1982.*

"The older people used to carry water from the stream in ollas but by the time we were of age, we had water pumps." Adelaide remembered carrying her baby sister, Jerry, to the spring on her back in a pouch made with her shawl. Jerry and Reycita used to fight over who would bring in the wood or whose turn it was to do the dishes. However, everyone was involved in spring cleaning, which began in May.

Aunt Shine also remembers:

They showed their love in such a quiet way. I don't know how to explain it. But you could tell, you know, that they had love for all of us. But, you know, they were not the type to go and start hugging everybody that comes in. They were just not raised that way. Just very quietly showed their affection.

[*] Our family is so close and shares and helps one another.

Maybe that is why we are so close, too. [*] And I think that is what our parents taught us, you know: to share what we had. Any time that we butchered a cow or sheep, then we would take the stew or meat to our relatives. So we shared with them.

And when they kill the deer, they invite everybody. Take food and the deer meat to relatives. So early in life we learned to share. There was always giving all we had. [*] We didn't have much but I think what we had we shared.

[*] We helped Dad farm and when morning comes it's "Get up!" We didn't say "Wait, let me do this first." Now, that's what you hear: "Let me finish this first." We didn't say that. We got up and went out. We don't talk back.

When asked what she would like children in coming generations to remember, Jerry replies:

They should learn to respect everybody. That people should respect themselves. And to respect the youth, their peers, everybody.

And not have to follow all the bad things that are being done nowadays. Many are into drugs and alcohol. They commit suicide. [Recently] a young man committed suicide. And shortly after, the wife committed suicide.

Those things we just never heard of because we seemed to live in such peace and harmony in our days and we didn't worry about anybody doing anything bad. We slept outside during the summer. Didn't worry about anything! Maybe frogs and snakes [laughs]. We watched the fire flies. You don't see this any more.

"I Would Rather Haul Hay in September . . . Than Sit in the Classroom!"

Schooling was always difficult—and fraught with federal politics. Each one of the family received different schooling that reflected the governmental policy toward Indians at that particular time.

Mother went to St. Catherine's Indian boarding school in Santa Fe for a short time. She understood English but couldn't speak it. Dad went to school in a small house behind the church. Father spoke English and Spanish and could read and write. He had a very nice handwriting. He read Spanish too. But when we went to school, he wouldn't talk English in front of us.

The daughters' rigorous and loving education in the ways of the Pueblo world was paralleled by their equally rigorous, harsher education at the San Juan Day School, set up by the federal government. Each of the five Cruz sisters attended. At that time well beyond the outskirts of the village, the one-room school covered the first four grades. Jerry began school at age seven, and she disliked it intensely:

I don't know at what age I started school—most likely at the age of seven. I didn't speak English, nor did most of the children, so we spent two years in kindergarten and pre-first before entering first grade. I was always happy to stay away from school. [*] I would rather haul hay in September or pick corn in October than sit in the classroom!

[*] We had a couple of very mean teachers so I was not too happy about school. All the teachers were Anglo then. The teachers were all good—well, not all. We had one teacher who taught math and if we didn't understand problems, she pounded our heads with a big turquoise ring she wore on her finger to get us to learn math. Another male teacher had a regulation "education board" that he used regularly to paddle the boys. He would also throw rulers, erasers, or chalk—whatever was handy—clear across the room if we misbehaved. And one day, the whole class ran away and we hid in the irrigation ditch the whole day!

[*] Adelaide and Pie completed eighth grade [at the Santa Fe Indian School] but didn't go on because the parents didn't let them go to another school and told them they'd had enough of school and it was too far. But they had a good education. They learned more than I did in twelve years.

[*] I tried all sorts of stunts to try to get out of the fourth grade because I didn't want to go away to school. I didn't want to leave San Juan.

(LEFT) Jerry (left) and her sister Reycita, ready to leave for their first day at the San Juan Day School (1922?). Family archives. (RIGHT) Jerry sitting between older sisters Piedad (left) and Adelaide on the steps of the San Juan General Store. They are waiting to be taken to the Santa Fe Indian School, 1927. Family archives.

Fifty years later, Jerry would transform the small school building she so disliked as a child into the first arts and crafts cooperative the pueblos would know.

Despite her best intentions, Jerry was unsuccessful in her attempts to fail school, and soon it was time for her to leave the center of her world—family, village, ditch, fields, and Rio Grande—and travel to another: the Bureau of Indian Affairs boarding school for Indian students in the city of Santa Fe.

PLATE 1. *Jerry dancing in Comanche Dance, June 24, 1977.*

PLATE 2. *"Basket Dance" Ground earth colors, 1934. Jerry's earliest extant painting. Jerry painted this as a student in the Studio at the Santa Fe Indian School. Dorothy Dunn Kramer purchased it and the painting hung for many years above her fireplace. Photographed with permission of Etel Kramer.*

PLATE 3. *Jerry participating in Basket Dance, January 1978.*

(ABOVE) PLATE 4. *"Under the Portal." Abstract design in shiva casein by P'otsúnú, 1979.* (BELOW) PLATE 5. *"Curious Young Turkey." Shiva casein by P'otsúnú, 1977.*

PLATE 6. *"Longhair Kachina." Shiva casein, brayer method, by P'otsúnú, 1977.*

PLATE 7. *"Geometric Pattern." Shiva casein by P'otsúnú, 1982.*

PLATE 8. *"Geometric Design." Shiva casein by P'otsúnú, 1977.*

(ABOVE) PLATE 9. *Crucita Cruz's pottery in front of the horno used for bread baking behind the "summer" house, San Juan Pueblo.* (BELOW) PLATE 10. *"Abstract Bird." Shiva casein by P'otsúnú, 1966. Photo taken with permission of private collector.*

2
A DAY IN THE WAGON
The Santa Fe Indian School

"Americanizing" the American Indian

Only three years before Jerry's arrival at the Santa Fe Indian School (SFIS) in 1927, the U.S. government passed legislation recognizing Indians as its citizens. However, another twenty-one years would pass before Indians in New Mexico were recognized as legal citizens of the state. This situation colored the treatment Jerry and other students received at school.

By the 1880s, most Indian tribes had been forcibly relocated or herded into barren reservation areas. These tribes, including those of New Mexico, had been promised government schools. The federal government, however, parceled out responsibilities for the earliest reservation schools to various competing Christian denominations. The missionaries' purpose was primarily to convert the "heathens" and then to civilize them by teaching them reading, writing, and arithmetic. Not until the turn of the century did federal support of the mission schools end in favor of government day schools begun on the reservations.

A few government boarding schools were established, carefully located far from reservations so the students could return home only occasionally. The military model for these boarding schools was based on the philosophy of Captain Richard Henry Pratt

37

whose post–Civil War experience in Florida with Plains Indians prisoners of war led him to found the first off-reservation Indian school, Carlisle, in Pennsylvania, in 1879. The plan was to separate children from parents and native cultures so that they would become quickly assimilated into the dominant culture. The government decided that teaching these children English, Christianity, and the virtues of honest labor would best prepare them for eventual citizenship.

In 1890, a coalition of federal government and Santa Fe business people built the Santa Fe Indian School, patterned after Carlisle and with the same stringent methods for acculturation and assimilation. Students boarded and were forbidden to speak their own languages, to wear any of their traditional clothing, and to participate in any ceremonial observance. The objective was to force children to conform to a distant government's dream of what an average and "good" American school child should be and value.

Tsianina Lomawaima, in her history of Chilocco Indian Agricultural School, points out that, in contrast to their goals, the "schools often strengthened rather than dissolved tribal identity" (1994, xiii). Still, many American Indian boarding-school children also retained or fought inculcated feelings of shame at their origins for the rest of their lives. Antonio García, the San Juan choir leader, commented: "It's still something I have to fight myself: that feeling of being a second-class citizen because I'm Indian. And much of this was instilled in the boarding school education."

In 1928, the Meriam Report, a government study of Indian administration, recommended new directions for off-reservation boarding schools. Among the recommendations were to raise standards for selecting teachers and to revise the curriculum to better fit the needs of the students. Under Indian Commissioners Charles J. Rhoads and John Collier, Congress increased appropriations to the schools and emphasized education.

A new superintendent, Chester Faris, was appointed to the Santa Fe Indian School in 1930. Faris' Quaker background well fitted the Pueblo way of working together cooperatively. Even the physical campus reflected transition. Many of the old, Eastern-style red brick

The family wagon in which Jerry was driven to the Santa Fe Indian School. Piedad is driving. Family archives.

buildings were remodeled under the direction of architect John Gaw Meem to reflect the style of buildings in the pueblos themselves.

Jerry's Boarding School Experience

Jerry, like all the other children at the Santa Fe Indian School, was a boarding student. To travel from San Juan to Santa Fe and the Indian School meant a day's wagon journey; trips home were rare. She arrived at the school when she was eleven and remained there as a student for eight years.

Jerry's experience as an obligatory member of the Indian School community was her primary contact with Anglo culture. If her parents provided a deep spiritual, emotional, physical, and cultural connection to Pueblo life, the Santa Fe Indian School enabled her to experience and participate in the Anglo world.

The government plan behind the school was to supersede the

early Indian acculturation with experience of the dominant culture. What the educators had not bargained on—certainly with Jerry and her sisters—was the Pueblo capacity to embrace apparently paradoxical perspectives without denial, conflict, or inner division. Jerry both fully embraced her way of life at the boarding school and left not one particle of home life behind. While she was a fine academic student, participated to the fullest in every school activity, became a school community leader, and learned Anglo language, culture, and manners flawlessly—to the government, a successfully assimilated American Indian—she was "just pure Indian," as she was later to describe herself: her ties to the Pueblo world were not even frayed, let alone severed.

If anything, Pueblo training in childhood made it easier for these children to make it through this alienating experience. They knew already how to help others, how to put their own needs second to those of the community; they knew well how to treat their elders with respect, and their parents had often admonished them to cooperate. According to one early student of the Santa Fe Indian School: "The attitude our parents gave us at home was, 'Don't ever forget your heritage. This is what you are and you can't ever change because you are this. But you must learn this other [culture], which is necessary in this life'" (Hyer 1990, 8). Robert Montoya, Jerry's oldest son, confirms this of Jerry, "Mother had a phenomenal ability to assimilate without loss of herself."

A crucial real and symbolic thread linking Jerry's two worlds was art. Dorothy Dunn, her art teacher, had long realized the value of allowing her young Indian students—most likely bound for unimaginative, government-determined, blue-collar occupations—access to their imagination, home life, and cultural heritage through art work. It was art and symbol that would allow Jerry and her classmates to transcend the duality of their Anglo and Indian worlds, to be both in school and at home, experiencing their ever-developing spiritual and cultural identity within their new Anglo setting.

Jerry speaks more about how boarding school opened new worlds for her than about her own feelings about the stringent rules. Her approach to this, her first major life crisis, reflects not only the strength and security she had gained through her family and culture, but also the strength and creativity in adversity that would later characterize her adult life.

"I Sure Was Homesick."

Neither of her older sisters was there to help Jerry make the transition from Pueblo to institutional world. Adelaide and Piedad had been sent to the Indian School by their parents but had already finished eighth grade there—the extent of education offered at the time—and returned home, where they were needed to help with the chores. According to one of the girls' dormitory advisors, "Indian parents . . . said, 'We send you to learn. This is a white man's world. We have to obey his rules. So you learn it when you're little.' And that was the philosophy the parents gave the children" (Hyer 1990, 6–8). Jerry remembers:

> I was in the fifth grade. I didn't know what I was doing. But I sure was homesick and lonely and I had hay fever so bad! One day, tears were running down my face from crying or from hay fever. I was sitting up in the front seat and the teacher, Rae Seibert, seeing me, came over to comfort me. She put her arms around me and that felt so good. My hay fever and the homesickness both just seemed to disappear. I forgot my loneliness. [*] From then on I studied and enjoyed my education. Miss Seibert was a very good teacher. [*] I corresponded with her and she wrote to me every Christmas until her death a few years ago.
>
> Being there the first time was kind of strange. [*] There were quite a lot of students from San Juan who were there. The first time they sent us away to school, they brought us by bus. Other times, my parents traveled by wagon to visit us—also at Christmas or when school was out, they came to take us home in the wagon. [*] When we first went to the Indian School, we had to stay the whole year.

According to Sally Hyer's oral history of the school (to which Jerry contributed several similar recollections), many of the children attempted to run away. This was one of the three main "sins" that the students could commit, the others being speaking their own languages and defying the school schedule. Children would run away usually because their homesickness was intolerable, especially when ceremonials were being held in their villages or when they could stand the institutional food (and lack thereof) no longer. Punishments were severe and public (1990, 14). Jerry was not immune:

> We ran away from school once and got as far as St. Catherine's Indian School. We went through Rosario Cemetery, which is next to the school. Anyway, we got as far as the cemetery and we were so scared that we started to pray out loud. We could see the monuments, and if someone had come out from behind one of them, I think we all would have dropped dead! The nuns at the school took us in but they immediately called our school and we were soon picked up to return to the school. The next day we were punished. We had to scrub the administration building, inside as well as the outside. They punished us for two days.

"We Marched to Everything!"

The school was run like a military establishment relying on severe discipline, punctuality, competitiveness, a hierarchical authority structure, and uniformity—of dress, language, behavior, and action. The military emphasis made a deep impression on Jerry:

> It was like a military school. We were divided by "companies." "A" Company would occupy a certain dorm and "B" Company would occupy another dorm. We didn't have individual rooms. Our beds were just close together.
>
> We slept in dormitories out on a long, glassed-in porch with forty to fifty girls. In winter there was no heat and it was terribly cold. When it got cold we'd double up to keep warm, and then, when we heard the officers coming, we'd rush back into our own beds until they were through checking. If we got caught, we'd get punished. Punishment was kneeling in the hallway. Not saying prayers, just kneeling.
>
> We had to get up at five or so. One of the boys would play reveille

on the bugle in the morning and taps at nights. We wore uniforms; boys dressed like soldiers. We'd march over to the main office to salute the flag after roll had been called. We would march on the lawn. We had older students for officers, and they kept us in line. It seemed strange to us. We marched to everything—to program, to the dining room, and to the church.

We wore uniforms—skirts, high-laced and tight black shoes, black stockings, red sweaters. We were tough, I guess, because all we had were sweaters to wear for winter.

The insistence upon marching was repealed by the Faris team some time after he arrived in 1930, five years before Jerry graduated. However, as Hyer notes, any of those children who had been earlier exposed to the marching often remembered it more than they did the academic portion of their day (1990, 11).

"They Didn't Allow Us to Speak Indian."

Language intervention was crucial to the school aim of divesting these children of their first cultural affiliation. Although most of the children arrived at the school knowing no English, punishments were severe for speaking the language of family and village. Students were tutored and had to catch up on the run.

The language policy, like the marching policy, changed after 1930 (Hyer 1990, 31). But the impact of the early years stayed with Jerry:

[Téwa was] the only language we knew at the time because we didn't know any English. We didn't have T.V.'s or papers or radios, so all we talked was the Téwa language.

[*]I didn't know any [English] when I first went to the Day School [at San Juan] so they spent a couple of years teaching us how to talk English. It was two years before we got into first grade. That's the reason so many of us graduated when we were much older. Now the graduates are much younger.

At SFIS they didn't allow us to speak Indian. Our gathering place was the locker room, where we would talk Téwa and sometimes we would dance.

"The Trunk Room Would Just Smell Like Melons."

If the locker room was a relatively safe place to speak their native tongues, it was also a good place to share food from home. The government-issue Anglo food was inferior, boring, foreign, and in short supply as far as the children were concerned. It also carried none of the emotional warmth or good memories that their home food did.

In the fall, when we returned to SFIS, we brought trunks—footlocker trunks—and they'd be filled more with food than with clothes. Chile and bread, melon, boiled eggs—things we couldn't get. And the trunk room would just smell like melons because everybody had them.

[*] The time that we went to school we didn't have money. There was a candy store across [from] the school and Cecilia [Bernal] had a nickel and she bought a Good Bar at that store and she shared the candy with me. She gave me one half and she had the other half and was standing against the wall of the gym and she said, "Hm! This is good." I always remember Cecilia that way. At that time a candy bar was a nickel. We didn't have money when we went to school. And now they come to school with ten, twenty dollar bills.

[*] The dining room meals were served family-style. Turnips and parsnips were served daily, and to this day I still hate them! In the dining room, the girls were all on one side of the dining room and the boys were all on the other side. By the time we got to high school we were allowed to mix and eat together.

"We Worked Half-Day and Went to School Half-Day."

Because of poor government funding and the attempt to inculcate the American work ethic, the school required the students to work at various unpaid occupations.

The whole student body were assigned to various jobs. Like the boys worked in the farm, in the mechanics shops, power house, the dorm, kitchen, bakery. And the girls were assigned also to the dining room, kitchen, hospital, to the dormitories. You helped the cook or helped in the dining room, helped with the dish washing. I think it was good experience for all of us. We didn't have things like that in our home, so this was an experience that I think everyone really got something out of, working in the various places.

When we were in the sixth or seventh grade, we were sent to the sewing room where we had to mend socks and more socks—laundry baskets full. You took one look at those baskets, you wanted to die. I guess this helped pay for our board and room.

[*] In later years, we worked half-day and went to school half-day. They changed us around. "A" Company would go to school in the morning and worked in the P.M.; "B" Company would go to school in the afternoon. The next semester it was vice versa. I worked at the U.S. [Public Health Service] Indian Hospital which was located next to the gym and helped the nurse treat emergencies. This nurse was tough and strict. We spilled iodine one time and she made us clean it all up with ether. Boy, that place smelled! We were really careful after that. I also worked in the laundry, the sewing room, and the kitchen, but I enjoyed the hospital most. I almost went into nursing. I appreciated the experience and training I received at the hospital. I liked working with the patients.

[*] Alvin Warren was one of my teachers either in the ninth or tenth grade. He advised us about the future: education and vocation. He had us write to colleges for bulletins. I sent for a nursing school catalogue. I was really interested in nursing because I liked what I did at the hospital. About the same time, school started to offer arts and crafts and I got interested both in crafts and painting and I stuck with those courses.

Jerry's interest in Indian art was first kindled in these arts and crafts classes, and they were to become of vital importance to her personally and professionally.

The American Indian Exposition and the Trip to Atlanta

The first major recognition of Jerry's expert community leadership, adaptability, and self-reliance came in 1934, just as she was entering her senior year.

Seniors stayed one month in the "practice cottage," where we took turns cooking and doing household chores. There were four of us at a time in the cottage. I'd cook one week, then I'd clean the house the next week. In September, the girls that were with me at the cottage had a surprise birthday party for me. At the party I was told that I was selected to go to Georgia. I was really surprised! Mary Belle Prowell, the home economics teacher and Practice House resident, announced it. I was so surprised and excited! Miss Prowell is Indian from Oklahoma.

Jerry had been chosen to travel to the American Indian Exposition at the Southeastern Fair, in Atlanta, Georgia; she was one of a small group of Indians from many different tribes invited at the special request of the U.S. Commissioner of Indian Affairs, John Collier. The group included María and Julian Martínez, the already well-known potter and painter from nearby San Ildefonso Pueblo; Martín Vigil, who would become a leader of his pueblo, Tesuque; Velino Herrera, whose paintings of Zia Pueblo would become highly prized; old Manuelito, a Navajo medicine man and sand painter; and Jerry's cousin from San Juan, Isabel Cruz. Other tribes represented were Seminole, Cherokee, Comanche, Kiowa, and Hopi. The Indian artists traveled for nearly four weeks through sixteen states and the District of Columbia in a cavalcade made up of three motor cars, a school bus, and a pickup truck. The Indian School superintendent, Chester Faris, and his wife were among those who accompanied the group. The tour lasted from September 23—one day after Jerry's nineteenth birthday—to October 18. As she noted at the time, "We traveled altogether a distance of 4,800 miles, a total of 24,000 miles for all the vehicles, approximately the earth's circumference at the equator!"

The significance of the event in Jerry's life is underscored by the fact that she kept a diary. For the first few days, she notes only the places through which they traveled: Tucumcari, New Mexico; El Reno, Oklahoma; Paris, Arkansas; Selmer, Tennessee; Dalton, Georgia; and finally Atlanta, where they arrived on September 28 with a police escort. Jerry was to later comment on their security:

One evening, Isabel and Josephine and I wanted to go out and eat at a nearby restaurant. Someone reported us to Chester Faris. He told us if we didn't get enough to eat at dinner to tell him but not to go out at night. He was concerned for us and we understood.

On Saturday, they readied themselves for the Exposition, and on Sunday the Fair opened. Jerry was to recall later:

After we finished the dances on the first day, we met Commissioner John Collier. On Wednesday, we danced in the fairgrounds. We did Belt Dance and other dances. On Thursday, we danced again but on Friday it rained. Then Saturday and Sunday, the last days of the Fair, we danced again.

Her diary relates the trip home:

Monday, Oct. 8
Finished packing. About noon went into the city. Filled cars with gas & oil & started for Washington D.C. at 12:30 o'clock. Stayed at Franklin, N.C. Visited Monticello, Jefferson's home. . . .

Wednesday, Oct. 10   Washington, D.C.
About 5:30 went to Washington Tourist Camp. We were invited to a dinner at the Department of Interior Bldg. by the Government employees.

Thursday, Oct. 11
Visited Abraham Lincoln Memorial, the Capital and the White House. Met Mrs. Roosevelt at the White House. Visited the Zoo. Got ready for an Indian dance at the Department of Interior Gym. Program at 8:00 pm. Isabel & I giggled over flash picture they took of us & couldn't sing. After a fashion we got started. We were very apologetic & Mr. Faris was so understanding & said it was all right [because people that don't know Indians believe that Indians don't laugh; he said that Indians can have fun and laugh (comment added 1994)]. . . .

Saturday, Oct. 13
Started for home at 10:00 a.m. Went as far as Pennsboro, W.Va. Old Manuelito left his medicine bag at the hotel that night.

(ABOVE) *Participants in the trip to the American Indian Exposition, Southeastern Fair, Atlanta, Georgia. Jerry is seated left. The potter María Martínez, of San Ildefonso, is standing third from the left. Sitting second from the right is Manuelito, the Navajo medicine man. Family archives.* (OPPOSITE) *Academic Building, Santa Fe Indian School campus. Family archives.*

Sunday, Oct. 14
Started from Pennsboro, W.Va. Had car trouble. The truck had to be towed about 15 miles to Parkersburg. Had breakfast there & had truck fixed there. We crossed the Ohio river & paid at the toll bridge. Stopped half a day waiting for Ambrose Roan Horse, Mr. Faris & Mr. Thompson. They went back to the hotel at Pennsboro for Manuelito's medicine bag. We ate walnuts, chestnuts, and hickory nuts while we waited. About 1:00 p.m. started on journey again. . . .

Tuesday, Oct. 16
Traveled all day & camped at Emporia, Kansas where Mr. Faris spent his birthday. Had a flat tire.

Wednesday, Oct. 18
Started from Lamar, Colo. about 4:00 am. Had breakfast at Trinidad, Colo. at 10:00 a.m. From there it was a non-stop to Santa Fe. Arrived in Santa Fe at 5:00 p.m. All safe.

The trip made a deep impression on Jerry and she considers it one of the most important events of her school life: "Since I never went out of New Mexico, the trip was very educational, exciting and a new experience. [*] Meeting Mrs. Roosevelt was a thrill. [*] The trip was one of the highlights of my school days."

Meeting Juan

Jerry was not solely preoccupied with her school schedule. By the time these older students were getting ready to graduate, they were permitted to socialize, and Jerry met the young man who would become her husband. Juan Montoya came from the southern pueblo of Sandia. Slim, handsome, and soft-spoken, Juan had a ready and kind sense of humor, which Jerry always enjoyed. Jerry explains how he and another friend from Sandia Pueblo, Pula (Esquipula) Chávez, came to the school:

> Pula's wife, Cecilia [Bernal], was just telling me when we went down to see her after Pula passed away: she said that Juan and Pula just ran away from Sandia and walked to Santa Fe to the school. They wanted to go to school so they just took off from Sandia and ended up at the Indian School.
> I think they ran away because someone didn't want them to cut

their hair; they wanted them to have long hair. Well, they didn't want to have their long hair, so they ran away [laughs] and I guess they got themselves all set up at the Indian School.

Jerry is brief about her first meetings and growing friendship with her future husband: "We met in school and that's it [laughs]." When asked if she remembers her first official outing with Juan or how they came to get married, Jerry replies: "No—I never think about those things. We just started going together."

"I Was in Too Many Activities."

The same Faris-born spirit of openness, inclusiveness, and reform that had abolished marching and encouraged arts and crafts also encouraged multiple extracurricular activities. Students could select from a variety of sports including archery, tennis, boxing, baseball, basketball, and track. Club options ranged widely: Boy Scouts, home economics, glee club, Indian club, student councils, band. "We had plenty to do. We had dedicated teachers who sponsored clubs. They weren't worried about overtime or holiday pay."

Some students, like Jerry, didn't choose among the activities; they tried to participate in them all. If the spirit of service and community responsibility had been ingrained in Jerry as a small girl at home, it was reinforced daily at the school. A lifelong pattern was seamlessly woven by now: a habit of taking on any task she deemed important.

In my senior year, the girls' advisor, Mary Bonn Fay, said I was in too many activities and wanted me to drop some of them and she even wrote to my parents and told them that I was spending a lot of time in the evenings at meetings. I was active in P.E., archery, and tennis. We had dedicated P.E. teachers who weren't looking for overtime. I was a Girl Scout, president of Hecha Kewa, the Happy Home Club, and helped with *Teguayo*, the annual class-funded senior year book. I was in the Glee Club, Dramatic Club, and Midewiwin Society, the Indian club. The advisor told my parents that I might have a

*Jerry, 19, on her graduation as valedictorian, Santa Fe Indian School, 1935.
She made the green suit she is wearing. Family archives.*

nervous breakdown and wanted me to drop some of the clubs. But I
just got a lot of joy out of being active and learning.

She did not break down. Now nineteen, Jerry graduated with honors from the Indian School, was valedictorian of the class of 1935,
and received the Dendahl Award for Outstanding Student. She was
the first in her family to become a high school graduate.

The Cruz family, on the day of Jerry's graduation from the Santa Fe Indian School, 1935. Left to right, back row: Adelaide, Piedad, Reycita, Pablo, Crucita, and Jerry (holding diploma); front row: Pauline, Ramoncita, and Queen. Family archives.

I made a green suit in sewing class for graduation and also a formal dress for the prom. I liked sewing then but now you can't get me to sew! I can't thread a needle for anything.

At the end of the school year my father and mother came in the wagon to get me and some of my cousins. We left school very early in the morning and reached the river at Tesuque in time to have a quick snack and then lunch at Pojoaque. We arrived in San Juan around four or five in the afternoon.

3
TRUE TRIBAL TRADITIONS
The Early Years of the Studio

Dorothy Dunn and the Philosophy of the Studio

The history of the development of traditional Indian painting is complex. Changes in policy at the federal government level, individual visions, and personal interactions all played vital and inseparable roles. Appreciating Jerry's commitment to Indian painting requires some knowledge of these powerful forces, which resulted in her assuming one of the primary individual roles in this process.

In 1928, after considerable investigation, the Institute for Governmental Research, a committee appointed by the Secretary of the Interior, criticized educators' failure to encourage the arts. Commissioner of Indian Affairs Charles J. Rhoads appointed W. Carson Ryan to come up with a plan for more tribally sensitive education (Dunn 1968). The superintendent of the Santa Fe Indian School, Chester Faris, with his multicultural awareness, provided rich ground in which to sow new educational seeds.

The Santa Fe Indian School was designated to pilot a new curriculum for teaching indigenous arts and crafts. In 1932, the school catalogue stated the new goals:

Organized to serve the general needs of future Indian citizens and the special needs of Indian boys and girls who desire to become craftsmen and artists.

When the Spaniards first came to the Southwest the Indians were subsistence farmers. They produced the food they ate. Today they do the same. Those who do this alone lack the growth in ambition and living standards which come with an added source of income such as an art or a craft. . . .

. . . The [school] should aid in reviving and preserving Indian art in an active way which will increase in value as time goes on. (93 DDK)

The following year, the new catalogue added the arguable comment that those Indians who were secure in their farming capacities had much free time and that

this free time is the key to fuller material and spiritual rewards thru the revival and encouragement of native arts and crafts towards which end this school is working. All pupils participate and have their appreciation of the beautiful nourished and enlarged thru an acquaintance with that which is their own. This should lead to happier lives. (93 DDK)

By this time, classes in over a dozen crafts were offered in addition to drawing and painting and design. The next year, the catalogue included a complete statement of the philosophy of painting and design, highlighting the importance of tribal traditions and the exclusion of European painting traditions.

By teaching students traditional arts and crafts, the school was reviving and affirming individual tribal traditions and providing a possible new form of work for graduates, whose opportunities for further education and decent jobs were limited and whose chances of self-sufficiency in village life had been reduced by their long absences at school. The students responded to the arts and crafts program enthusiastically; in their villages, arts and crafts, were part of everyday life.

The curriculum was not the only structure transformed: so were the buildings. A new arts and crafts building was opened in 1931.

In 1932, under the supervision of Olive Rush, the respected Southwestern painter, a few students and several older artists from San Ildefonso—many of whom were sponsored by the Indian Division of the Public Works Art Project—painted the first of a number of murals at the school. The students painted those first murals in the drab dining hall where they had reluctantly eaten so many turnips. The result was outstanding. Rush showed unusual sensitivity in helping these young artists render their imagination onto walls, believing that "this is a precious thing, and he must move softly among them that would help them adjust their art to our modern world" (Dunn 1968, 245).

Rush showed the artists how to use materials that were new to them and made suggestions that she hoped would enhance rather than deflect her student painters' natural predilections in content and style. She also helped the artists cooperate to realize their vision. Olive Rush was a special presence in the students' lives. Jerry remembers her: "A tiny woman. She was very pleasant—and smart. Quiet, very understanding, kind as she could be. She was a very good artist. Her work was so simple and just so soft. She could be aggressive too."

Beatrice Chauvenet, artist and art historian, also remembers Rush well:

> Miss Rush was a slight woman but she had strength and determination. She admired the American Indians and their art and gave them technical advice on the painting of frescos. She painted the murals in the old Santa Fe public library and in the dining room at La Fonda but she stays in my mind for her watercolors of animals, chiefly deer. . . . Her paintings are delicate, sensitive.

Although the murals were complete and had received widespread acclaim and encouragement, the Arts and Crafts Department still had no painting classes. Edgar L. Hewett, educator, archaeologist, and director of the School of American Research in Santa Fe, also encouraged the expansion of the curriculum, maintaining that:

> the purpose now is to broaden the experiment by extending the

same opportunity and encouragement to other individuals and tribes until it is made a fair demonstration of the ability of the race and the possibility of reviving a power that has been submerged, dormant through generations. (Dunn 1968, 249)

At the same time that the federal government was de-emphasizing assimilation and encouraging tribal awareness and pride, Dorothy Dunn was evolving her own individual vision for Indian art. Dunn's memories of the Studio's development are important for several reasons: she initiated the Studio's intent and operations; she documented its development in minute detail; and she significantly influenced Jerry's philosophy as an artist and teacher.

Dunn had studied at the Art Institute of Chicago where she became most interested in Indian art during anthropology classes and classes at the Field Museum. She pursued her new passion independently, researching what meager material was available, and after graduation found herself a teaching position right in the center of the area whose art so fascinated her. She taught for two years at Santo Domingo Pueblo and for one year on the Navajo Reservation.

"[In those years I] found more Art than I had ever dreamed of in Chicago." About this time Miss Dunn met Mr. Kenneth Chapman,

(OPPOSITE) *Olive Rush supervising students from the Studio who were paint-*
ing murals in the cafeteria, 1932. Family archives. (ABOVE) *Students and*
staff of the Santa Fe Indian School, standing in front of the completed din-
ing room murals, 1932. Left to right:————, *Riley Quoyavama, Ed Lee,*
Olive Rush, Raymundo Vigil, Superintendent Chester Faris, Jack Hokeah,
Rush's assistant Louise Morris, Albert Hardy,————, *and Richard*
Martínez. Family archives.

noted Indian art authority in Santa Fe, who opened up many new
vistas and showed her sketches of drawings of leaf forms from the
pottery of a single pueblo and these seemed to symbolize to her the
infinite variety and richness of Indian Art. During these days Miss
Dunn worked incessantly in the basement of the Art Museum [of
New Mexico, now the Museum of Fine Arts] with the Indian Arts
Fund Collection. Here she sketched books and books of design and
so became acquainted with the designs of the different tribes.
Attendance of all the ceremonials and acquaintance with all the
important archaeological sites were another part of her practical
training. She says, "There was so much to learn that it was almost
overwhelming, but I never had felt so completely at home in the
world before this." (J. Rehnstrand, "Young Indians Revive Their
Native Arts," *School Arts*, November 1936, 137–138)

According to her own narrative account, the ground was now fertile for Dunn. She put forward her proposal to create a painting studio to be incorporated into the Santa Fe Indian School. Chester Faris was quite open to the concept, but at this time in the Depression, he could obtain little funding for a new position. Being an astute civil servant, he was not deterred: he suggested to Dunn that she apply for the position of fifth-grade teacher and then, with the aid of some "odd labor" funds, develop the Studio in addition to her regular teaching. Dunn accepted the challenge. She knew exactly what she wanted to achieve:

> 1) to foster appreciation of Indian painting among students and public, thus helping to establish it in its rightful place as one of the fine arts of the world . . . 2) to produce new paintings in keeping with high standards already attained by Indian painters, 3) to study and explore traditional Indian art methods and productions in order to continue established basic painting forms, and to evolve new motifs, styles, and techniques in character with the old and worthy of supplementing them, 4) to maintain tribal and individual distinction in the paintings. (Dunn 1968, 252)

She was equally clear-sighted and passionate about her methods. She wanted to "determine, insofar as possible, each student's personality, interests, abilities, the backgrounds of his tribal art and its relationship to his individual art and the general arts" and, "without teaching in the formal sense, to create a guidance technique which would provide motivation, clarification, and development for each individual student's painting process" (Dunn 1968, 252). In a draft of a paper written presumably for educators' eyes, Dunn spoke further about the function of design and painting classes: to search "for the new to be original"; to develop the capacity to differentiate between "gaudy sketches in the curio shops and the refined ones in the permanent collections"; to approach "the highest standards of the race by using fine products as examples" and to "never [use] European-American criteria except in cases where they are big enough to be universal"; to create discerning markets; to use museum collections intelligently; and to "discover talent and encourage art work where it might not take form otherwise." Moreover, Dunn wanted her students to have an appreciation of their own tribal art and to see that in some ways it was superior to Western art (93 DDK).

Critics and artists, both Indian and non-Indian, have taken strong positions on several of the issues she raises here: Can a non-Indian teach American Indians something about their own traditional art forms or help them realize possibilities for new art forms without contaminating them with European values, processes, media, and influences? What does "traditional" mean within each discipline—art, ethnography, anthropology? And what do American Indians mean when they use the word "traditional"?

Dunn believed that "Indian painting is the first art in history to have sprung, full-fledged, from the primitive into the contemporary world at a time when it was peculiarly compatible with both" (Dunn 1968, 24). This is a romanticized version, certainly, of what Dunn actually had to do to foster the talents at the Indian School. Nothing sprang full-fledged in these students. And the belief that American Indians as a "race" were "naturally gifted" in the arts echoes the theme of the undiscovered noble savage waiting to be awakened by the enlightened European. The mural experiment with Olive Rush, however, did undeniably demonstrate that there were highly talented artists among the school population who, given even minimal encouragement, would be able to explore and realize their abilities.

Dunn's determination to exclude or discourage foreign influences was too late, ultimately, given the heavy acculturation to which these students had already been subjected in the content and style of their education. However, Dunn believed that limiting the academic influences and encouraging freedom of expression would allow the original talent to emerge. She was as determined to create a nonconformist, non-assimilative environment as those in the decade before her had been to create a conformist, assimilative one. In an article for *School Arts*, "Indian Children Carry Forward Old Traditions," Dunn describes this challenge:

Before a great number of the student artists acquaint themselves with the public they must first understand themselves. It is for these frustrated, groping, inhibited ones that the school functions most of all. They must be dealt with individually, slowly, understandingly, and cautiously lest they close entirely and never open. The undesirable, alien influences must be totally destroyed before even a simple correct beginning can be made, but they are often difficult to overcome because of reticence or pride or the human unwillingness to change. (March 1935, 428, 93 DDK)

Dunn was not alone in her vision. Influential people, in addition to Olive Rush and Kenneth Chapman, strongly supported her: Rose Brandt, the supervisor of Elementary Education of the Bureau of Indian Affairs, in Washington; Frederick H. Douglas from the Denver Art Museum; Gustave Baumann, the eminent Southwestern artist, and his wife; and Margretta Dietrich, at that time president of the Southwestern Association on Indian Affairs.

Most of these people visited the Studio on a regular basis. Jerry remembers their visits. Her descriptions of them are purely in response to our specific questions. As she said, "I guess I'm not very interested in people's private affairs." She does recall that

Olive Rush and Margretta Dietrich were always helping [around the Studio], quick about doing. [*] Margretta Dietrich was tiny, too, like Olive and she was aggressive like Olive. Margretta was around the Studio more than Olive Rush. Margretta was always purchasing paintings. She was interested in Indians in general I think.

The realization of Dunn's vision was a daily exercise in versatility and improvisation. She faced logistical, financial, and educational problems: she had little time in her teaching schedule; she had little money for art materials; her room was inadequate; and the curriculum was tight and formalized, even under Faris. Ironically, her students were, by now, so trained to expect a structured, non-Indian curriculum that they were at a loss and disconcerted, initially, when Dunn encouraged them to explore their own directions.

They were still unused to including anything of their Indian culture in their school lives. Moreover, their acculturation to the dominant culture had pervaded their sense of aesthetic and understanding of what "art" was. Art was so pervasive and unspoken in their villages that to think of its being a separate entity—"art"—was a leap in conceptualization, an act of acculturation in and of itself (Dunn 1968, 254).

Dunn saw herself as an artist-researcher and guide, not as a formal teacher. She spent much of her early time at the school observing the students' choice of subject and style that emerged without any guidance. She recalls that she continued in this way until Mabel Morrow, the head of the Arts and Crafts Department, voiced concern over the lack of formal training being provided in art. In response, Dunn experimented with models and portraiture. The experiment was successful only with a few older students.

Shortly thereafter, with her program rapidly growing in popularity, she moved the Studio to larger quarters, enrollment doubled, and Faris allocated two half days for painting per week instead of one. Dunn and the students celebrated the expanded opportunities by painting murals in the new Studio.

For Jerry, her arts and crafts studies marked the beginning of her lifelong passion for traditional creative expression.

Under Mabel Morrow I studied weaving and embroidery. I also spun my own cotton and wove a white manta in the Hopi style. The embroidery was on handwoven cloth and monk's cloth. Dying wools for weaving and embroidery with natural dyes was another subject I took. I also learned carding, spinning, and washing wool, beadwork, basketry, Indian games, songs, and dances for recreation and camp work. We learned how to select clay and sand, how to make pottery and fire it. Miss Morrow sent me out to Nambé to teach crafts as part of my training in crafts.

Dunn, by this time, was able to offer Jerry a variety of experiences. Jerry used the transparent watercolors and tempera that were available and experimented with Dunn and the rest of her fellow students with color mixing, intensity, and values. She learned how to work with different qualities of brush lines on manila paper. She also learned how to work with pencil, charcoal, and chalk, experimenting with "pictographic life drawings of circular, elliptical, [and] angular elements" (Dunn 1968, 258).

Dunn continued to discourage outside influences on her students' work:

> Any production which revealed copy of unworthy exotic influence was discouraged, not by forbiddance, but by suggestion of a variety of choices of tribal elements which might make a particular painting more authentic and interesting. . . . If non-Indian and out-tribal influences might be intelligently used after the young artists were well familiar with their own tribal source materials, the decision to do so should later be in the hands of the artists themselves, particularly after they had left school. (Dunn 1968, 261–262)

She elaborated on this concept of originality in the draft of an article, "American Indian Painting," she wrote for a British publication, the *Civil Service Arts Quarterly,* 1936:

> Very unlike other arts which have held sway so long in the Western World, American Indian art stands apart for its lack of eclecticism. [The] Indian artist chooses the subjects nearest his experience, his daily occupations, his simple home life, his ceremonials, and sets them down in strong yet delicate patterns of pure, flat color. Sometimes his interpretations reach pure abstraction in symbols of sun, clouds, falling rain, and plant growth. In no instance is the Indian artist a copyist or a naturalist; he is always a poet and an interpreter. His attitude toward painting is much the same as that of the Chinese painter; he knows his subject thoroughly and then, without model, records his thoughts with decisiveness and directness. (93 DDK)

Considering what she said later in her own book, it might have been more accurate for her to say that students had to be educated not to take their precedent from other traditions and that moves toward derivative art were strongly discouraged rather than absent.

Around this time, Dunn wrote a brief update on the aims of her art program at the school:

> The Santa Fe Indian School, through its art classes, is attempting to recover and develop America's only indigenous art. Much of it has

been irretrievably lost, of course, but Indian art students are delving in forgotten places, searching through ethnological papers, studying museum collections, inquiring of their elders, making observations for themselves from what remains of the old cultures, and reconstructing their racial heritage as a basis for building new things which will contribute to America's cultural progress. They find that, although their subject matter is different, the outcomes of their efforts do not differ greatly from other modern art developments. (93 DDK)

Dunn also discouraged copying from other students, believing and teaching that "to copy from one another was unethical but . . . to raise the standard of one's own work to equal that of the finest painting on display was a worthy effort" (Dunn 1968, 275).

Around this time, she also began to encourage the students to do murals using native materials—clays, sandstones, and color-bearing ores from all over the Southwest. Together, the students gathered, prepared, and named the ores, sandstones, or clays for their origins. Dunn probably realized that preparing materials from their natural habitats was a process most of her students knew, understood, and respected. Since she was a baby, Jerry for example, had seen Yíyá, her mother, collect and prepare the clay for her pots. The process of grinding color must have seemed much more natural than using color from tubes or blocks.

Under Dorothy Dunn, then director of Fine and Applied Arts, I studied Indian painting in the true, tribal traditions. The media I used were watercolors, tempera, oils, and native earth colors. I also painted two murals. Dorothy purchased the one painted in earth colors; the other mural was painted on linoleum with oil paints. [*] I don't know where it is now.

Dunn seems to have wanted Jerry and her fellow students to have the experience of working with both indigenous and European art materials. Whether the earth media were more "traditional" does not seem to have been an issue. Their selection was a result of exigency as it was of aesthetic or ethnic influences; during the Depression these were affordable media.

Some critics have argued that, from the moment that non-Indians introduced Indians to non-Indian materials, "traditional" Indian art was contaminated and therefore not really traditional. However, others, like Gerhard Hoffman, hold that "only if Indian art is seen as a changing art can one accept that it need not lose its genuineness when it adopts a foreign medium" (in Wade 1986, 258). Certainly, this was the position that Dunn and her students took.

Jerry and her classmates also had the opportunity to contribute paintings for an annual May painting show at the Museum of New Mexico. Olive Rush reviewed the show in *El Palacio*, at that time a free weekly review published by the School of American Research in conjunction with the University of New Mexico and the Museum of New Mexico. *El Palacio* was sent to members of the New Mexico Archaeological Society and to Santa Fe and Albuquerque societies of the Archaeological Institute. The director of the School of American Research, Edgar L. Hewett, was most interested in and supportive of the work at the Indian School. In her review, Rush praised Jerry's basket dance painting:

> A San Juan girl, Po-Su-Nu, has a Hopi basket dance done in earth color on native ground. The design is a fine achievement through simplest means, one great sweep of line for the shoulders of her women, and a clever use of triangles, circles and straight lines for developing her theme. ("Exhibit of Indian Paintings," *El Palacio*, 1934, vol. 36, nos. 20–26, 200)

As the Studio entered its third year, its success, according to Dunn, created logistical problems. Jerry—new to the Studio that year—and her classmates helped Dunn move the Studio into the old, vacated library. They bought supplies using money they had earned from sales of their paintings. It was a year of exhibits, commissions, and new murals for the social science room, although the students could hardly find the time for all the work. They made frenzied preparation to send posters to the Musée d'Ethnographie in Paris to accompany a show; Dunn reported that Studio members and other students enjoyed this challenge and worked intensively for two days.

That year, their May show was again well received. It was reviewed this time by Frederick H. Douglas, Dunn's supporter from the Denver Art Museum, who commented that "the exhibit of Indian water-colors on display . . . is . . . an extremely inclusive setting forth of this remarkable modern art development." Douglas thought the exhibit "prove[d] conclusively that the inborn artistic gifts of the Indian race are strong enough to have survived the attacks of bureaucracy and civilization and to emerge stronger than ever in its new generations" and evidenced the "ability to move forward instead of crystallizing into certain well mastered forms. . . . New forms are ever appearing" (Dunn 1968, 281–282). Dunn must have been pleased by his comments, given the students' tentativeness in those first days of her art classes three years earlier.

If Jerry had seen something special to be learned from Dunn over these three years as the Studio developed, Dunn also had seen something special in the leadership potential of her young, serious student, Jerry, who was just about to graduate. "I liked her very much. She was quiet, stolid. She could stand her ground like Gibraltar." Yet Dunn, like other teachers, worried about the cost of Jerry's activities to her health. "She was very slim. Her last year she had gotten too thin—like a sliver" (personal communication). Dunn also saw something special in Jerry's art, commenting later: "Po-Tsunu . . . painted in a similar way [to T'o Póví, Lorencita Atencio] with broader, stronger brush treatment and less emphasis on small design. Her art was placid and decoratively literal" (Dunn 1968, 292).

When Dunn invited Jerry to stay on at the Santa Fe Indian School as an apprentice teacher after her graduation, Jerry's acceptance probably signaled not so much her desire to develop a career as her heartfelt response to a request from a woman whose work and whose person she deeply respected. Jerry wanted to be of service. This was a way to serve and earn needed money to contribute to the family.

A Teaching Career

Indian art before World War II resembled the town of Santa Fe itself: not easily accessible, remote from direct European influence, its source of life and inspiration derived from the high mountain desert. The small Anglo community housed many Western artists whose works would later be famous; in the same way, the Indian School community included many young student painters whose work would later command respect and good prices. Into this ripening and political world of American Indian art, Jerry Cruz moved, no longer student but fledgling teacher and artist.

Teaching art represented a coming together of many influences on Jerry's life: her parents' emphasis on education and tradition; her commitment to Pueblo spirituality, ceremony, and community; her Catholic commitment to service; her Pueblo traditions as they could be rendered in artistic form; and her Anglo training in duty and academic excellence. So it is not surprising that Jerry took to teaching with a clarity and commitment that were stronger than her shyness and reticence. She would give decades of vision and creativity to the evolution of Indian art and nurturing to young, homesick, talented Indian artists, many of whom went on to become leaders in the field.

Jerry completely affiliated with the way that Dunn taught and Kenneth Chapman and others viewed Indian art. Indian art was not art for art's sake alone for Jerry or for her mentors. It was a twin, second born, to the experience of cultural identity, preservation, and life. Art it was, without question, and it received homage as such from an increasing number and variety of sources, but it was always subsumed to the service of collective Pueblo values, values that placed community above individual, balance and tradition above achievement.

The twenty-three years that Jerry spent teaching art at the Santa Fe Indian School were often troubled by policy and politics. Still, while she agreed that we might, if we wished, include our less than positive findings and opinions about how she was treated at the school, she, herself, wanted to say "nothing negative; it's all past and gone now."

"I Was Pleased but Kind of Scared at the Same Time."

The summer of 1935 brought changes. Chester Faris left the school and was replaced by Superintendent H. C. Seymour. One Indian School employee remembers him as being "kind of a typical Easterner, very businesslike, not very friendly, a bit of a dictator. He'd come around early in the morning and talk with everyone about what they were doing" (personal communication).

That same summer Dunn, who had long before recognized Jerry's leadership and artistic potential, placed her in charge of the earlier grades in the Studio.

Because the majority of painters had already worked in the Studio, there had grown a fine rapport between student and student and between student and guide. New students were received by everyone with helpful attitude. The younger beginners had a class of their own this year with a graduate of the Studio, Geronima Cruz (Po-Tsunu), of San Juan Pueblo, assisting. (Dunn 1968, 284)

That summer, Jerry took additional courses in health at the school.

We had summer school after I graduated in '35. Then in September, I think, Dorothy asked me if I would like to work with her teaching the seventh and eighth graders. I was just assigned to take over. I don't know who made that decision, whether she did or whoever was in charge. I was pleased but kind of scared at the same time. I said I would do it—with her help and her guidance. So that is what I started to do right out of high school.

Her new teaching assignment in the fall of the fourth year of the Studio, 1935–1936, consumed most of her time and marked the beginning of her teaching career, which was to last for thirty-eight years.

Dorothy left a lot up to me. I followed what she did with me— followed in her footsteps. She was a wonderful person to work with—encouraging. She made things easy for me. It didn't take me long to get used to it, working with her and knowing the students. So many of them are from our pueblos that I got acquainted with them and then their parents. So it was easy in that way.

I started to work with Dorothy in the Studio. I just took art. But Mabel Morrow was the crafts teacher and the two of them—Mabel and Dorothy—were fighting over where I should be! Mabel Morrow wanted me too. And of course I helped her out—like an apprentice teacher. We went out to the pueblos—San Juan, Nambé, Tesuque, and Santa Clara—to teach.

At that time, I don't think there were any other Indian teachers. But the craftspeople were all Indians. I think Mr. Roan Horse was already there because I remember some of the pictures that he was in with his silversmith boys. And George Blue Spruce was teaching woodworking. A lot of the Indian people worked in the kitchen and maintenance too.

I taught Indian painting to beginners—color, figure drawing, brush work, and charcoal. I received a salary of 840 dollars a year under Miss Dunn's supervision.

Dunn was very fond of her youthful companion and assistant: "Her English was good and she showed obviously fine leadership qualities as she worked with the beginning students" (personal communication). Dunn was also delighted with the cooperation and support among the students:

> The older members seemed as interested in the work of these younger artists as in that of their own age and experience level. Beginners felt free to go to others for advice if they wished. Everyone belonged.
>
> Guidance techniques had evolved into an assumption of mutual understanding between student and guide wherein, for the older students, a minimum of suggestion was necessary. (Dunn 1968, 284)

This was an exciting year for Dunn: she had an assistant to help her with her younger pupils and the time to prepare basic motifs from different tribes for presentation in class. She also had the cooperation of several museums who either made their materials available to her when she visited them or sent materials to the Studio.

Such source material was studied by the classes for authenticity of spirit and style, for veracity of small detail, and for skilled control of media as well as for historic content. It was never copied outright by the students other than for study, but its influence was allowed free play in the creation of works following and improvising on traditional idioms as a springboard to future developments. (Dunn 1968, 283–284)

That year Kenneth Chapman also lent the support of the Laboratory of Anthropology by coming to the Studio. The Laboratory of Anthropology was now part of the Museum of New Mexico and was, in the thirties, a unique teaching and research organization dedicated to the study of Southwest Indian cultures and the preservation of their art. The Laboratory began to help stem the flow of irreplaceable art to Eastern collectors. Chapman presented students with material on American Indian painting, also evoking particular interest, according to Dunn, in Egyptian, Mediterranean, Persian, and Chinese art styles.

Jerry remembers Chapman well as "a knowledgeable person. He was tall and slender. His main interest was Indian art and pottery. He was a good teacher." She, too, took courses from Chapman to improve her own art background:

In 1935 and '36, I took two extension courses in Indian art from the University of New Mexico, given by Kenneth Chapman at the Laboratory of Anthropology. I took "General Indian Art of the U.S." during the winter evenings in 1935 and '36, and a summer course in 1936, in Southwest Indian art. [*] I guess I loved school. Every time there was a school, I was there.

This fourth year, 1936, was for Dunn the most rewarding year for the Studio. The annual show exhibited over six hundred paintings and received high praise from many, including Annette Fassnacht, an educator-anthropologist:

Has Indian art at last arrived? It is, rather, that we have at last become able to appreciate an art so mature as that produced by the Indian artists. . . .

These artists have proved that they can venture outside the field of ceremonial life and still keep within the traditions of their art. (Dunn 1968, 289)

Dunn seemed particularly pleased by Edgar L. Hewett's comment to her: "You are heading in the right direction. . . . This painting is new, but it is Indian" (Dunn 1968, 290).

The two guides went into the fifth year of the Studio believing that not only was the school watching them now but also the public; their success had nudged them into the politics of the art world and the education world.

Dunn saw trends developing: "tribal, sectional, and individual" (Dunn 1968, 290). In the Pueblo artists, she saw conventions being established, such as preferences for ways to paint certain animals and aspects of nature. She also saw the beginning of abstract design by younger students whom Jerry was teaching. Shifts in color preferences were emerging. Perspectives began to resemble those in the paintings of the cultures that Chapman had shown them and that had evoked their interest: Egyptian, Mediterranean, Chinese, and Persian. Certain Pueblo subject matter, however, seemed to be avoided for tribal reasons. Again, Dunn asserts that "there were no

The Studio of the Santa Fe' Indian School cordially invites you to attend its fifth annual exhibition of paintings at the Museum of New Mexico and at the Studio, May first to fifteenth.

The Studio of the Santa Fe' Indian School cordially invites you to attend its fifth annual exhibition of paintings at the Museum of New Mexico and at the Studio, May first to fifteenth.

(OPPOSITE) *Acoma design drawn in pencil by Jerry during a class with Kenneth Chapman at the Laboratory of Anthropology. 93 DDK, Laboratory of Anthropology, Museum of Indian Arts and Culture.* (LEFT) *Jerry, sitting on the bank of the acequia in San Juan, 1937. Family archives.* (RIGHT) *Jerry's hand-printed invitation to the fifth annual May exhibit of paintings from the Studio. 93 DDK, Laboratory of Anthropology, Museum of Indian Arts and Culture.*

rules and nothing was ever said about these limitations; they were simply recognized and respected within the Studio" (1968, 291).

In 1937, exhibits were sent to over thirty different destinations including the Museum of Fine Arts at Stanford University and the Second National Exhibition of American Art at the Rockefeller Center in New York. The Studio painters' reputations were soaring. Olive Rush was delighted for them all and for the implication for the larger art world. Her review was included in *El Palacio*'s article on the show.

A continued amazing development in the art of painting by the students of the United States Indian School at Santa Fe, under the direction of Miss Dorothy Dunn, is again evident in the magnificent exhibit that has been on display recently in the art museum and at the studio of the school. . . . Their work demonstrates a native ability that might well be the envy of a very great many of our Anglo-American art students. Yet this Indian work remains an indigenous art, as distinctly Indian as the Pueblo pottery.

Miss Olive Rush, the well known local artist who has given unstinted aid to this unique development, wrote the following review of the show for the *Santa Fe New Mexican* . . . :

It has been a delight the past week to go into the state art museum where an art so different in aspect from our own blossoms and glows upon the walls of two alcoves. Is it great art? We are led to so believe from these examples. . . .

. . . Through the work of youth from 11 to 20 there is not a trace of carelessness, and no lack of keen observation. Not an exhibit here but is arresting in its own happy way.

Rush concludes the review by mentioning Jerry's young students' work:

Assisting Dorothy Dunn, director of the department, who so ably guides the work to keep it purely Indian and uncommercial, is Jeronima Cruz of San Juan, a former student who has charge of the younger pupils. At the studio, there is an entire roomful of the work of her pupils, excellent in standard for children so young. ("Annual Indian Art Show," *El Palacio*, 1937, vol. 42, nos. 19–21,105–108)

"I Left for Good." (Dunn)

At the end of that year, the Studio was awarded the Médaille de Bronze at the Exposition Nationale des Arts et des Techniques in Paris. Then suddenly, Dorothy Dunn and the school parted ways. What is publicly known about this is that she married the school science teacher, Max Kramer, and moved to Taos where Max took an appointment as principal of the Day School. When she spoke with us in 1978 about her departure from the Studio, she appeared passionate, guarded, and sad about what she experienced as injustices, miscarriages, and misinterpretations, which remained alluded to yet veiled during our conversation together. "I did not make children do Indian art. They wanted to. My encouragement has been vastly misunderstood by critical people."

Dunn's last spring and summer at the Studio were unhappy and beleaguered. In early March, Dunn was dealt a blow when she walked into the classroom of her future husband, Max Kramer: the exquisite science murals that the students had painted were gone. Also erased, throughout the school building, were the ceremonial murals and home life murals. In their place was a layer of government-regulation house paint. Devastated and outraged, she wrote to Seymour. In his reply, the superintendent held himself "partially responsible since I did not specifically point out to [the painters] what should be and what should not be painted out." He went to on document his attempts at damage control: by the time he had reached Max Kramer's room, too much of the mural had been painted over to save it, so he ordered the rest painted over; when he reached the dining room, he was relieved to see that at least the murals there had been covered up only with wall board. He stated he was extremely sorry about the event, suggested Dunn check on the safety of the murals that were left, and suggested that new murals might be painted from old photographs. Dunn must have found the letter cold comfort. Seymour had responded as though she had told him that she had found her most precious possessions robbed because he, as a guest, carelessly left her house unlocked. The note of apology and equivalent of "I'm sure you must have insurance" did nothing to assuage Dunn's loss and anger. As she wrote to her supporter Rose Brandt:

The most recent blow to our studio was the discovery that our science murals and the ones in our old studio had been entirely painted over last week. The architect assured me last fall that they would be protected. If I should stay on another year, I'm sure I would find myself back at the point where I began in 1932, except for the paintings which are away from here in places where people care for them, and for the few students who may carry on. All the propaganda I read about the wonderful things the Indian Service is doing are a grotesque joke to me. If anything worthwhile is being done, . . . I know it is being done by individuals who are bucking tremendous odds, not by the Indian "Service." (93 DDK)

Compounding her sense of her work being undervalued was her belief that she was underpaid. In April of that fifth year, Dunn wrote to the superintendent asking for either her first salary raise in four years or a fully trained associate to assume half of the responsibilities. Although her letter outlined some carefully crafted options for resolving the gap between her passionate and boundless involvement with the Studio and the low wage, she saw this situation as more than a sin of administrative omission; after several paragraphs discussing the responsibilities she was carrying, she concluded with the undoubtedly accurate but unwise comment:

> And in just what form should I inform the Director of the Budget that I am quite willing to dispense with all titles and continue my work at twenty-two hundred per annum [up from $1860]? After all, that is little more than the rating of a civil service awning maker.

Later that month, Dunn raised questions with Seymour about her two teaching assistants' status. Seymour again replied in a long, detailed letter articulating the value he placed on her and her assistants' work:

> I do not imagine you have a great deal of time to produce paintings, for the reason that your time is occupied solely in teaching and in managing the studio. I myself feel that even though you have artistic ability, your work in teaching students to develop their own ideas in art and techniques for creating pictures of merit is of greater service, since your personality and ability affect a great many students. . . .
> . . . You seem to indicate that Jerry Cruz and Lupe Sando have not been given enough credit for their work. As I told you . . . I have made recommendations to Washington for re-allocation for Jerry Cruz. . . . [but] the government way of handling appointments . . . is a slow one. (93 DDK)

Jerry and Virginia Bailey, her faculty roommate, waiting in Claremont, California, for the 1:41 P.M. overland (train) to Santa Fe, 1937. Family archives.

Perhaps one reason Dunn was concerned about Jerry's recognition was Jerry's ill health. It was only two years since everyone had been concerned about Jerry's having a nervous breakdown from overwork. Now she was again unwell. Possibly they feared tuberculosis, which was widespread on the reservations. Dunn wrote to Rose Brandt:

> Both Jerry and Virginia [Bailey, Jerry's roommate] are back at work again. Jerry's X-ray disclosed no difficulty but she is very, very thin and colorless. I hope she will go home for the entire summer and live in the sunshine and grow strong and rosy like she used to be.

In the midst of this unhappy time, a young man came to visit the Studio during the summer. Lloyd Kiva New had graduated from the Art Institute of Chicago and wanted to talk with Dunn about job possibilities. Dunn did not like him: "I remember clearly and have carried the image over the years of L. New wandering into the Studio that summer. . . . His face was broken out. . . . He [was] arrogant, sallow, and morose. . . . I recommended Phoenix [Indian School] to him" (93 DDK).

Dunn had, apparently, an intuition of dissonance between New and herself. The implications of this awkward exchange were enormous; it was to be this "arrogant, sallow, and morose" young man who, at the Indian boarding school in Phoenix, would develop a rival school of painting with a radically different philosophy— an art movement that, twenty-five years later, would fell the Studio with a single, well-aimed political blow.

The rest of the summer brought no relief for Dunn professionally, although it was during this time that she quietly married Max Kramer. She resigned in August, shortly before school was to begin, and went to live in Taos with Kramer. Her champions, Margretta Dietrich at the Association on Indian Affairs and Kenneth Chapman at the Laboratory of Anthropology, were surprised and supportive. Dietrich, on learning of the news indirectly, wrote to Dunn immediately:

> It was the first I had heard . . . and I felt perfectly sick. . . .
>
> I went up in the afternoon as soon as I could get away from lunch to see Chap [Chapman]. It was the first he had heard, too, that you had left. . . . He says that as soon as he can he will write to . . . the Rockefeller Foundation . . . asking whether [it] would like to contribute to make it possible for you to carry on what we would call "adult education" among the graduate students and older Indians.
>
> Chap feels sure you could have an office in the Laboratory.
> (93 DDK)

Apparently, Dunn was not relying on anyone to find her work. In her official resignation letter, she spoke of needing "greater freedom" to develop Indian art and of applying for a position with the Arts and Crafts Board of the Indian Service. Discussions with Kenneth Chapman and René d'Harnancourt of the Arts and Crafts Board ensued. Willard Walcott Beatty, director of education at the Bureau of Indian Affairs in Washington, was also, apparently, going to discuss with Dunn the possibility of developing an art school (93 DDK). In October of 1937, Dunn wrote to a friend:

> When I left the Santa Fe school this summer, I left for good because I couldn't stand the present political regime there any longer. I left

the studio in the hands of a San Juan girl, Jeronima Cruz, whom I had trained three years as a student and two years as a teacher. She is exceedingly capable, and, being an Indian, she may be less interfered with than I was. Things finally got so bad that the harder I would fight for the right things, the worse they would become. I'm now trying to get a position directly under Rene d'Harnancourt . . . which would take me into the Pueblos and Reservations to work with the artists and craftsmen themselves without the tremendous handicap of petty local authorities who know nothing about art and very little about anything except cheating and lying and bluffing. (93 DDK)

Dorothy Dunn Kramer never returned to teaching. During the war years, 1941–1946, she moved with her husband and daughter, Etel, to many parts of the country, always writing articles and doing research, which culminated in the publication of *American Indian Painting* in 1968.

While Dunn's own energies for working within what she experienced as a hostile environment were spent, her attachment both to her twenty-one-year-old successor, Jerry, and to the Studio remained strong. She urged her friends and colleagues to support Jerry, whom Seymour had agreed to appoint. The mantle of responsibility and politics that now fell on Jerry's shoulders was historically heavy. Furthermore, Dunn was Anglo and had some sense of government politics, a strong art education, and connections. Jerry was twenty-one, a minority on the predominantly Anglo teaching staff, and a trainee teacher only two years out of high school. The situation was strafed with political cross fire.

"I Was Promoted to Head of the Art Department."

Regardless of whether the full story of Dunn's resignation is known and understood, the impact of her departure on Jerry was resounding. Jerry says she knew nothing about the details of this upheaval. It was a complete surprise to her when she accompanied us to the Laboratory of Anthropology to review Dunn's newly archived records. Prior to our visit, all that Jerry said was that in 1937, Dorothy Dunn resigned. Her husband, Dr. Max Kramer, had been our science teacher and now was going to be principal at Taos Day School, so they went on and moved up there.

I was promoted to head of the art department. My salary was raised to twelve hundred dollars. My duties were the actual teaching of Indian art to students in grades seven through twelve.

Jerry remained in close contact with Dunn. She wrote to her to ask for guidance and encouragement when political and educational turns of events seemed overwhelming or untenable.

"In October of that year, I was given my first formal invitation to lecture. I addressed the Art Section of the New Mexico Educational Association [NMEA]." This invitation to speak was a first for Jerry, and she wrote to Dunn for help.

Dunn apparently encouraged Jerry to create her own material. A report of her lecture suggests that Jerry spoke from her own education about the art of other tribes and then spoke from personal knowledge of the Southwest and her teaching experiences. In beginning to integrate Dunn's art education with her personal tribal knowledge, she was coming to trust her own capacities as artist, teacher, and commentator in the field of American Indian art.

> Miss Jeronima Cruz, a San Juan Indian girl, teacher of Indian art at the Santa Fe Indian School, gave one of the most interesting talks heard at the art section meeting of the N.M.E.A. convention last week where widely different viewpoints in art education were expressed. Miss Cruz spoke on "Interpreting Indian Arts and Crafts," and, having lifelong knowledge of the subject, she gave some unusual information on this often misleading topic.
>
> Beginning with the generalization that art to the Indian always grows out of his daily life which is determined by his tribal environment, Miss Cruz followed with specific interpretations of Indian art in different areas. She explained the fish and animal motifs of the Northwest coast, the hunt and war influence in Plains art, the floral designs of the Woodland groups and, in clear detail, the controlling influence of climate in Southwest Indian art. . . .
>
> . . . Miss Cruz . . . is a member of the State Art Teachers

Association and the only Indian representative. (Iris Ellis, New Mexico Art Teachers Association, to the Indian School, undated)

As well as beginning to give talks to the public, Jerry was in contact with people in art circles in New Mexico and elsewhere, helping her students to achieve recognition from ever-wider audiences: "In addition to this regular art work, I selected paintings for exhibits. I had requests from leading art centers constantly and just couldn't meet the demand."

One of these "demands" came from Olive Rush. Olive invited Jerry to paint a mural commissioned by the owners of Maisel's Indian Curio Store in Albuquerque. To Olive's disappointment, Jerry refused, preferring instead to select some of her students to work on the panels alongside the established painters chosen by Olive Rush—Awa Tsireh, Pop Chalee, and Pablita Velarde. Today, the list of students who participated reads like a "Who's Who" of twentieth-century Indian painting: Quincy Tahoma, Narcisco Abeyta, Harrison Begay, Eva Mirabal, Joe H. Herrera, Ben Quintana, Wilson Dewey, Theodore Suina, Popovi Da, Henry Gobin, and Beatien Yazz.

Jerry's promotion brought other challenges less pleasant. As early as 1938 she encountered the inflexibility of government opinion, which ran counter to the art philosophy and style Dunn and now Jerry emphasized. About the same time as her successful talk to the New Mexico Educational Association, Jerry was criticized by Superintendent Seymour for not teaching the students correct values. He told Jerry that when students painted on outside time they should turn in at least 10 percent of the money from sales so that they would not be under the impression that they received materials for free. This was important because "Indians get everything free." She was further told that Indians were unappreciative and did not know how to trade, so contributing 10 percent was important for educational purposes.

When Jerry pointed out that the students were already contributing considerable sums for their supplies, she was told that the students still were using government lights, heat, and room. Jerry held her ground but the emotional cost was high. What kept her

Jerry with María and Julian Martínez on Treasure Island, San Francisco, during the 1939 Golden Gate Exposition. Family archives.

from walking out on the job was her belief in the importance of what she was teaching and her loyalty to the students.

The 1939 Golden Gate Exposition in San Francisco

When Jerry was only twenty-three years old, she took a school group to California to participate in the 1939 San Francisco Golden Gate Exposition, where a special exhibit of murals in the building devoted to American Indians displayed the work of the Santa Fe Indian School. Jerry and the other visitors lived at the Yerba Buena Center on Yerba Buena Island, a land link for the San Francisco–Oakland Bay Bridge. Some of the students who had painted the Maisel murals were there with them, as well as María and Julian Martínez, María's nephew Gilbert Atencio, Ascension Trujillo, José C. Herrera (Zia), Dixon Shebala and Roger Tsabetsaye (Zuni), and Charlie Lee (Navajo).

The foundation for a lifelong friendship was one of the rewards of the trip. Young Anita Montoya, also from San Juan Pueblo, was part of the company. Years later, Jerry and her husband would serve as godparents for the children of Anita and Popovi Da, the son of María and Julian Martínez and an illustrious potter in his own right.

"An Important Place."

By 1939, Jerry's experiences as American Indian artist and teacher had consolidated into firm beliefs, values, and practices. One of the students who benefited from her encouragement of tradition combined with individual style was Beatien Yazz, a young and brilliant man whose work later became widely known after the publication of Alberta Hannan's two books about him, *Spin a Silver Dollar* (1945) and *Paint the Wind* (1958), which Yazz himself illustrated. He was among the first Southwestern Indian painters to illustrate books.

Jerry's approach to American Indian art and its teaching was consolidated and interwoven with that of her mentor, Dunn:

> Work was developed from memory and from research and authentic records. As students progressed, each developed his or her own style and went at his or her own speed, and I gave individual instruction . . . . As art teacher, I taught American Indian painting because I believe that Indian art has a distinct and an important place in the art world. I encouraged and developed true tribal traditions in the painting classes.

4

THE TALENT
THAT WAS THERE

Family and Teaching

"A Traditional Woman."

Jerry has lived a life of unshakable commitment to tradition integrated with precedent-setting independent action. Raising a family while directing the Studio demanded that she embody this apparent dichotomy daily, perhaps more then than at any other time in her life.

American women at midcentury were not expected to begin families in their thirties. Even fewer with young children were pursuing college studies or full-time professional careers. The number of women from a nondominant cultural group—of any age—attending college or holding down professional careers was small. Mothers who were holding full-time professional jobs, sharing child rearing equally with their husbands, and pursuing degrees at the same time were rare. All of this is what Jerry did in the forties and fifties.

Jerry was not aware of her uniqueness, nor would she have been particularly interested in it. She never saw nor reflected upon the groundbreaking approach that she and her husband were taking to their life together and that she was taking to her own life as a woman. To this day, Jerry experiences and describes herself as a "traditional woman"—a woman with conservative Pueblo, Catholic,

(LEFT) Jerry, the year of her marriage, 1939. Family archives. (RIGHT) Jerry and Juan Montoya on their wedding day, August 26, 1939, at San Juan Pueblo. Family archives.

and educational values. Her uncompromising adherence to these values itself produced such radical action.

Jerry did not intend to develop a profession while raising a family, to be one of the first American Indian women to graduate from college, or to extend the boundaries of women's development in the dominant culture. She responded to circumstance. She was asked to serve as a Studio teacher, so she served and eventually became its youthful director. She expected to marry and she did. She expected to have children and she did. The children needed financing for a good education and the school still wanted her, so she continued to work. The school required more highly qualified teachers, so she went to college. She knew she couldn't do all this without the full support of her husband and extended family who lived with her—but she didn't know this was almost unheard of at that time for women, especially women from oppressed economic and cultural groups.

A traditional woman, in Jerry's opinion, responds to the needs of her family and community, and that was what she was doing. As Jerry would tell the students of the reinstated Indian School forty years later, she believed that contemporary traditional women should be strong, raise families, pursue higher education, participate in religious activities, serve the wider community, engage in lifelong learning, and preserve their culture (see Afterword).

Just as Jerry saw no conflict between Pueblo and Catholic religions, neither did she see conflict between traditional values and original action. Her steadiness of spiritual, cultural, and psychological identity allowed her to translate these values into action. In her heart, she was always loyal to the fundamental principles that informed her life.

"I Got Married Saturday Morning."

On August 28, 1939, Jerry wrote to Dorothy Dunn's mother, Mrs. Carpenter:

> Dear "Mom"—
>
> Just a short note to let you know that I got married Saturday morning, August 26 at San Juan. I married Juan Montoya, I can't remember if you met him at all, but you might have.
>
> Dorothy, Max and the baby came to the wedding, also Virginia [Bailey] and Fuzzy [Annette Fassnacht].
>
> I just got back to work this morning. I plan to stay at the Studio yet. For some reason I hate to leave the studio and the students I have had. . . .

When Geronima Cruz and Juan Montoya were married, Jerry had already been teaching for four years at the Indian School and Juan had been doing construction work on the Jicarilla Apache Reservation in Dulce, in northern New Mexico, for two years after graduating.

As is Pueblo custom, Juan chose the sponsors for their wedding to act as advisors or special parental figures for him and his bride and to help provide the feast. He chose his aunt and uncle, Margaret and Luciano Luján, from Sandia Pueblo.

The wedding took place at San Juan Pueblo, as Jerry wished, in the small Chapel of Our Lady of Lourdes, across from the church and in front of the Téwa rock shrine marking the world navel. Perhaps Jerry liked the intimacy of the chapel for this special occasion and wanted to invoke the blessing of the Holy Mother. Jerry's wedding dress was simple, classic, and white, with a full-length veil. Juan wore a dark business suit.

As Juan and Jerry said their vows, Pablo and Crucita stood with their oldest daughter, Adelaide, and her nine-year-old daughter, K'use' P'oe Kwîn (Antonita, or Queen). Beside them were Piedad and her Navajo husband, Bill Antoine, and their daughters, nine-year-old Pauline and infant Elidia. Younger sisters Reycita and Ramoncita looked on.

The Montoya family from Sandia watched quietly as Father Joseph Pajot performed the wedding Mass at ten o'clock that morning. Juan's parents—Andrés, a farmer, and Isabelle—and brothers, Adam and Domingo, had journeyed two days by wagon, ninety miles northward along the Rio Grande, to be there. It was the first and last time the parents of bride and groom would meet. Andrés was so ill with tuberculosis by the time the family returned to Sandia that he had to be helped down from the wagon. He never walked again. Adam, also suffering from tuberculosis, still widespread in the pueblos, died in December of that year. But on this cloudless morning, there was no sign of illness as the party returned to the Cruz family home and the great wedding feast.

More than two hundred people feasted that day—all of San Juan Pueblo was invited to share—waiting their turn to sit at the dining room table, consuming quantities of wedding bread, red and green chile, posole, salads of all kinds, gallons of cool drinks, and desserts of bread pudding, fruit pies, tarts, cookies, and wedding cake. Everyone ate without conversation—quickly, as Pueblo manners required, so that a place at the table would soon be vacant for another guest.

Two days later, Jerry and Juan returned to the Indian School where both would remain on the faculty for the next twenty-three years—Jerry as art teacher and then Studio director; Juan as woodwork instructor and school scoutmaster, taking generations of boys camping.

(LEFT) *Jerry, around the time of her marriage. Juan carried this photo in his wallet all his life. Family archives.* (RIGHT) *Jerry and Juan's house on the Indian School campus. Family archives.*

That first year of their married life saw joy interwoven with sadness. During the winter, they celebrated the marriage of Reycita to Charles Jirón from Isleta. But soon Piedad's husband, Bill, died from undiagnosed tuberculosis. The widow and her young daughters continued to live close to Juan and Jerry in Santa Fe, and Piedad went on with her work at the Public Health Service Indian Hospital, which adjoined the school campus.

Despite their sorrow at Bill's death, the family joined together again at San Juan to celebrate the marriage of the youngest sister, Ramoncita, just eighteen, to a Navajo man, Gilbert Sandoval, whom she had met at the Indian School when both were students.

"In the Art Studio We Work in a Democratic Way."

Jerry, by now, was building a strong reputation in the community as a talented and skilled studio director. In an undated document, "Education for Democracy," she described the daily applications of her philosophy in the Studio:

> Work is developed from memory and from research in authentic records. Our medium is Shiva casein tempera.

. . . All beginners studied the fundamental principles in art. That is, color mixing; color harmony; brush work and technique; drawing human figures—following the oval methods; chalk and charcoal drawing.

As students progressed, each developed his or her own style and went at his or her own speed and individual instructions were given. Some of the things covered at this time were block cutting and printing, textile printing and painting, drawing in pencil and India ink. Corrections and suggestions were made wherever needed. Correct mounting of paintings is emphasized and exhibitions are sponsored in the leading art centers of this country and Europe. Production cards were filled by the students for each picture they painted and they often helped with the pricing of their pictures. This way they learned how pictures are priced and will be able to price their own pictures later on.

In addition to painting we have had short courses in art appreciation. In that, we tried to cover the more famous paintings and famous artists. I have obtained prints of famous paintings which I showed. We studied art vocabulary and art materials—old and new. Posters, invitations, and programs for class parties were also made. A certain amount of this is allowed in class time so that they will have experience in doing other things.

In the art studio we work in a democratic way. Students are free to get up when they are tired and see what the others are doing. Very often the older students will help the younger students. They are free to get their water and clean their brushes and jars. They are free to view the pictures on exhibit and make comments and ask questions. They are free to use any type of paper they choose. The only time they need to ask permission is when they are leaving the building.

Jerry had many other responsibilities at the school, which she oulined in the same report:

I had senior girls in my home room and some of the things we discussed during this period were: grades; grade points; etiquette; ethics; difficult subjects—where and how they could improve. Time was also spent for class meetings: discussion of class projects, home letters, and self rating. Articles for their class night were written, that is, class history, class poem, class prophecy, class song, class will, class flower, class colors, class motto, etc. Plans for senior banquet, graduation and senior trip were also made during home room period. Rehearsal for class night was done at this time too.

As senior class sponsor, I held our regular class meetings monthly or as the need arose. I held private consultations with class officers and other senior members that needed guidance. Some of our extra projects for earning class money were sales of candy, food, and programs at games. Class carnival was held and a full hour and a half all Indian program. This, I felt, was one of our outstanding events. I felt that the students did a very fine job in their native dances and the "turn out" of the crowd was excellent. We also carried out a photography project in which the senior class received 25% of the pictures sold. The money raised went to pay for their rentals on caps and gowns, class rings, graduation announcements, appreciation gifts, extra things needed for banquet, and for their senior trip. . . .

. . . We were also responsible for getting our own speakers for commencement exercises. . . . I had fine cooperation from those students. I felt that my job was to guide them along and advise them only and the final decision was up to the seniors. For that reason they wrote their own letters and planned all other things as well, while I acted only as consultant.

Alfred Morang, a respected Southwestern painter, was to note Jerry's democratic approach to teaching art in his *El Palacio* review of the 1940 May show.

The art of the American Indian is closely related to the art of other races while maintaining its own individuality. . . .

. . . The racial element, at least to this writer, is transcended by the sheer art of these pictures. Of course the work is rich in tradition, filled with racial memories, but after all in most painters there are racial memories. . . . In some of these pictures by Indian students, the matter of balance is breath-taking.

Jeronima Cruz Montoya, the teacher, has a rare grasp of the problems involved. She does not force the work into any preconceived pattern. She obviously allows the student to project his own ideas upon paper, and simply guides him into a more rounded development of his initial creative impulse. . . . [This exhibit] should demonstrate what emotion guided into art can accomplish when it is not limited by academic standards. (*El Palacio*, 1940, vol. 47, no. 5, 117–118)

"People Who Would Oppose Us." (Dietrich)

While Morang had praised the show highly, Margretta Dietrich, still loyal to the Studio even after Dunn's departure, indicates that there were other concerns about the Studio work and a foreshadowing of the eventual demise of Studio even as early as this. In a letter to Dunn, Dietrich passionately relayed the negative critique given to the Studio work by a visitor.

> I was very much shocked when I went to the School Exhibit to have [Jerry] tell me—Chap told me a Dutchman had been around sent by [Willard Walcott] Beatty who objected to everything down in the Art Dept. at the S.F. School but praised Phoenix—Chap says the Phoenix work—landscapes & from models—in oils, is as bad as possible—He was there this winter—
>
> Gina Knee, Dor. Stewart [Dietrich's sister], Sara McComb & I are at this moment addressing letters to artists all over the state & many over the country—And I am writing to Museums where our collection has been shown—
>
> Could you take the Taos list or get someone there to do it for you—I don't know Taos artists & their attitude toward Ind. painting—We don't want to stir up people who would oppose us—
>
> I am taking the attitude that [Superintendent] Seymour is only acting under directions from above & would welcome our help—
>
> I asked Geronima if it would hurt her if we circulated these letters & she said no for if she had to carry out instructions she couldn't teach & the boys said the same. (93 DDK)

It seems, from additional correspondence in the Dunn archives, that Willard W. Beatty, director of education at the Bureau of Indian

Affairs in Washington, asked a Dutch photographer to visually document work done in the Indian Schools. Dietrich believed that Beatty was trying to undermine the Studio work, and as a result of her letter, Beatty was besieged by protestations. As he later said, in response to a letter from Dunn absolving him from any responsibility:

> As you suspected Sekaer the photographer was at the bottom of it with his totally unauthorized comments on Indian art. . . . The fact that Mr. Sekaer might have some explosive ideas about art or politics . . . was not evident in our preliminary interview. . . . That apparently coincided with an interview between Mr. Seymour and Jerry which upset Jerry considerably.

Apparently, Superintendent Seymour had shared his criticism of Jerry's teaching with Beatty in a meeting in Washington. Beatty continued:

> I suggested that he discuss them directly with [Jerry] . . . and unfortunately the discussion appears to have been fraught with misunderstanding. . . .
>
> . . . After all, I believe that I stand for exactly what you do in principle. It is difficult to find people who can carry out what we want. The process is slow and mistakes will be made. It is particularly unfortunate when those who believe themselves to be friends of the things we stand for put themselves in the position of throwing bombs within the home camp. (93 DDK)

While Dunn had made clear to Beatty that she believed, unlike Dietrich, that he had no intentional part in this mess, she was still appreciative of Dietrich's efforts on the Studio's behalf, commenting in a note typed on the bottom of Dietrich's letter to her:

> Jerry—Geronima Montoya—a San Juan girl in early 20s, was an excellent painter, lovely, conscientious, intelligent person, who had been my assistant a year, then successor. Supt. Seymour, a chief cause of my own leaving, had sole charge of the school which was

officially cut off, with all United Pueblos territory, from Wash. office. I knew Beatty could have had no official connection with SFIS at this time. . . . Mrs. Dietrich acted under high principled intentions always, and usually very wisely. In this instance, it seemed to me the Assoc. which she headed needed stronger evidence to act on. A thorough investigation then might have prevented more disasters rather than in some aspects promoting them inadvertently through the vindictiveness of reprimanded parties, one of whom Lloyd Kiva New proved to be.

It seems from Dunn's note too that, whether intentionally or unintentionally, the visiting photographer had aligned the Santa Fe and Phoenix schools opposite each other philosophically. It further seems that Dietrich managed to get Lloyd Kiva New reprimanded for whatever role he played in the criticism of the Studio philosophy and work. Given that he apparently felt Dunn had rejected him on his visit to her in 1937, his subsequent criticism of the Studio is hardly surprising. His vision of Indian art would become the chief opponent to the Studio's vision.

"My Job Was to Bring Out Their Talent."

Jerry's descriptions in an undated report written about what was happening in and around the Studio were less political, more pragmatic:

> Last spring I supervised mural painting in the Social Science classroom. . . . The wall was prepared by the students themselves. The old paint was scrubbed off with trisodiumphosphate solution and was painted over with Shiva casein colors. Domestic scenes are the subject. Apaches, Navajos, and Pueblos painted the murals. One of the girls is now making a sketch for a mural for [Superintendent Sophie D.] Aberle. This is to be done on canvas using Shiva paints and to be done under my supervision. The subject is Taos round dance.

(ABOVE) *Pueblo wedding mural by Joe H. Herrera (Cochiti) and Wade Hadley (Navajo). Family archives.* (BELOW) *Navajo life mural by Quincy Tahoma (Navajo). Family archives.* (BOTTOM LEFT) *Jerry consulting with Joe H. Herrera about a mural he was painting in the Studio. Family archives.* (BOTTOM RIGHT) *Quincy Tahoma (Navajo), working on a detail for a mural in the Studio. Family archives.*

Narcisco Abeyta (Ha So Deh, Navajo), working on a study for the Studio murals. Family archives.

In a much later description of her work, Jerry adds:

> Each student received individual instruction, as my job was to bring out their talent and have them draw and paint in their individual way and style while still keeping it Indian. Each one did his own tribal life.
>
> These children were trying to put their heritage down in a form which could not be distorted or misconstrued by outsiders. They were doing it for their own people as well as for others.
>
> In the twenty-seven years I taught in the Studio, my object was not just to perpetuate old forms but to study them, understand and appreciate them, and develop new forms related to and worthy of succeeding the old ones.
>
> Being an artist myself meant that I had to watch so that I would not do the drawings for the students. The biggest job was to bring out the talent that was there in the student.
>
> I had to prepare all the materials for my classes because there

were no textbooks on Indian art. I had to do a lot of research work on various Indian tribes, Bureau of [American] Ethnology reports, museum publications, photographs, and other material on home life, costumes and ceremonials, in order to be of help to students like Henry Gobin. At the same time, I gave the students proper guidance to keep originality in their work.

Jerry's student Henry Gobin, for example, knew little about his own people, the Snohomish of Washington, when he first arrived at the school. She helped him to research their history and background and find examples of their art. "Henry didn't know anything about art or his people. I used to sit and talk with him about what to do." Gobin would later become a well-known artist.

Ben Quintana's Prize and the Trip to New York

While many students, like Gobin, knew little about their own tribes, others brought to the Studio an understanding of and sensitivity toward their own cultural heritage. Certainly one of the most talented of these was Ben Quintana, from Cochiti Pueblo. Dunn later commented:

> Ben Quintana was one of the few who are so endowed that they might one day be masters. At twelve he painted Cochiti ceremonials with a sureness, dignity, and insight that already rivalled the work of artists conceded to be of top rank in Pueblo art. His varied subjects were taken from all walks of Pueblo life and interpreted with rare selectivity and beauty of brushwork. (Dunn 1968, 294)

When Ben was sixteen, Jerry entered his casein watercolor, along with works by Quincy Tahoma (Navajo), Ignatius Palmer (Mescalero Apache), and seven other students, in the nationwide 1940 *American Magazine* Youth Forum Contest, sponsored by Crowell-Collier Publishers. Of 52,000 entries, Ben's painting, *What My Community Contributes to the Nation,* won first prize. All of her students won awards juried by Dr. Everett V. Meeks, dean of the Yale University School of Fine Arts, Albert Lefcourte, art director

Ben Quintana (Cochiti), national prize winner of the American Magazine Youth Forum Contest, with Jerry. He was later killed in action. Family archives.

of *American Magazine*, and Norman Rockwell. Ben's award was one thousand dollars and an all-expense-paid trip to New York. As his teacher, Jerry also won the trip, along with one hundred dollars.

In Cochiti, the Quintanas, however, had great uncertainties about committing their son to travel so far away from their small adobe home near the southern Rio Grande. Jerry decided to drive out and talk to Ben's parents, finally locating them far from the village, in their summer quarters on the Cochiti Reservation, a remote and starkly beautiful area now submerged beneath the waters collected by Cochiti Dam. As she sat down with the Quintanas, the twenty-five-year-old teacher realized she had obstacles to overcome. First, individual achievement was not highly regarded in the Pueblo value system; then, too, she herself was young, a woman, and from a different pueblo, speaking a different language. Such were Jerry's powers of persuasion, however, that hours later the Quintanas gave their consent, and Jerry was able to return to the school with good news for Ben. Thus Ben, seventeen, began his first train trip, leaving Albuquerque for New York in Jerry's company.

For Jerry, neither her Atlanta nor San Francisco experiences were comparable to this extraordinary week. They stayed at the Biltmore Hotel, where they joined the other award winners and their teachers. Their tour of the fabulous city included Times Square, the top of the Empire State Building, Greenwich Village, the Battery, Wall Street, and the Stock Exchange. She would return every evening to the Biltmore exhausted and exhilarated, rising the next morning eager for more.

They ate at famous hotels—the Waldorf Astoria, the Astor—and went on an all-day boat trip up the Hudson River to see the military academy at West Point. They went to Broadway plays—*Life with Father, Louisiana Purchase,* and *There Shall Be No Night* were part of their itinerary. They went to Radio City Music Hall and to museums—the Metropolitan Museum of Art, the Museum of Modern Art, the Museum of the American Indian, and the Hayden Planetarium. One evening, they heard a concert by the New York Philharmonic, with Arturo Toscanini conducting.

This was not to be Ben's last trip away from home. He returned to New Mexico four months before the United States entered World War II and on his graduation from the Santa Fe Indian School was drafted into the Army. In 1945, at the age of twenty-one, he was killed in action in the Philippine Islands, far from Cochiti.

Ben's prize painting vanished. Jerry assumed his parents owned it until she learned from Ben's mother that they did not. Then when the Indian School was terminated in 1962, many paintings stored in the cellar and long-since forgotten were turned over to the Southern Pueblos Agency of the Bureau of Indian Affairs. People were allowed to come in and choose what they wanted for their office walls. Sam Arquero of Cochiti, a relative of Jerry's and an administrator in the agency, chose what later turned out to be the vanished painting. He hung it in his office, having no knowledge of the painting's prizewinning history but hoping at some time in the future to be able to free it from Agency ownership and return it to Ben's parents.

Philosophical Battles

Jerry now had a well-developed taste for travel, which she shared with her students. One of the longest group trips was with the Indian Club to St. Louis, to take part in the National Folk Festival. She also led field trips to art museums, the Laboratory of Anthropology, and the Museum of New Mexico Hall of Ethnology to do research work.

No matter what accolades and recognition were given Jerry and her students, however, the government educational policy continued to be that Indians were best suited to jobs involving manual labor. All through the late thirties, students continued to work hard to keep up with vocational course work. To make her courses more vocational, Jerry began incorporating sales and marketing methods.

> When a picture was finished, I helped the student figure out the cost of materials that had gone into that particular painting and after everything had been figured out I priced the picture. When we had a group of paintings finished and priced, we had our own exhibit in the studio where we kept them for a while. Afterward, we sent them to the arts and crafts sales room. These exhibitions gave the students a chance to see what others had done and make comparisons and criticism and ask questions.
>
> I was in constant contact with people outside of our Indian Service. We had foreign visitors to the studio all the time, and I had to show what we did and how it was done. We mingled with professional artists, curators of art museums, anthropologists, owners of art shops, and many, many people interested in Indian art.

Institutionally, internal difficulties continued despite the external success. In 1942, Jerry found herself in opposition to the philosophy and administration of the school. Her integrity held firm although heart and pride were deeply bruised. That year she received an "unsatisfactory efficiency rating," being unexpectedly criticized for not dividing her art teaching time into segments: one hour for lettering, one hour for design—what Jerry described in a letter to Dunn as "regular public school stuff." She was continually distressed, perceiving that truly creative work was no longer valued by most faculty.

Concerned that administrators did not know or understand Indians, let alone know what they needed, she adhered to what she believed was the educationally and culturally optimal teaching approach that Dunn had established, taking the risk of letting her peers think once again that she was "just a stubborn Indian." Still, she tried to be positive and find humor where she could, as this small extract from a personal letter to Dunn indicates:

> We have Dr. Whitaker, from Stanford University who is the Educational Director for the two schools. But he doesn't know the studio and he doesn't know me and I don't know if we have a superintendent. Doesn't the whole thing sound like Indian Service? . . .
>
> . . . I go to night school at Loretto taking typing and shorthand in case things go worse to worse—maybe I can get a job or something on that line, or at least be able to get in Civil Service through typing and continue with art.

That same year, she wrote to Dunn again, telling her about exhibits she was mounting and her attempt to overcome administrative obstacles to her marketing student work:

> We are having exhibits now at Fred Wilson's, Santa Barbara and Los Angeles. Next week we are sending out two groups to Nacogdoches, Texas, and Knoxville, Tennessee. That takes in about all the paintings we have. The first two weeks in April we are having an exhibit at the Art Museum [Art Gallery of the Museum of New Mexico] in Santa Fe. School is going to be out on the 30th of April so that is the reason we are having the exhibit so early. I am not supposed to write letters that are concerning exhibits, art, etc. It is all supposed to go thru [Mary] Mitchell but lot of times I go ahead anyway and write. . . .
>
> . . . The past two weeks we had an exhibit of Mrs. Dietrich's collection of [our] paintings here at the Studio. The kids enjoyed them so much. They looked at them for hours every day. It was certainly

good to see them again once more. I should say they brought me many happy memories. I put a poster up at the office inviting every-one to see it but only a few came.

It seems that Dunn was faithful about writing back to Jerry and encouraging her in what she was doing. She might also have dis-cussed with Jerry the possibility of working together again in some capacity because Jerry responded in late November of 1942:

I certainly will work with you any day, in or out of the Indian Service. I have never had, & never will have, a finer person to work for, work with, etc. etc. than you. I think of those days many times. . . .

. . . You will be glad to hear that I have been doing some paint-ing. I painted 4 paintings lately & sold all of them. It is kind of hard to paint at nights though.

If Jerry still missed Dunn, so did others, as Jerry's letter further indicates:

I saw Olive Rush at the Art Museum yesterday and she sends her love to you. She said she had been thinking about you and wonder-ing where you are, how you are and what you are doing. She was so glad when I told her all about you and Max. She is also disgusted with the way you & Max have been treated. She, too, hopes that you will all come back again to this school to take over. . . .

. . . Mr. Faris came thru some time ago & wants to be remembered to you. He asked me about you so I told him that you were in Illinois. He didn't know either Max was out of the Indian Service. . . .

Did you know that Narciso [Abeyta] is in the Hawaii[a]n Islands somewhere? Justino H. [Herrera] is in England somewhere, probably in Egypt by now. So many of the kids are across that for-merly came to the school here. I even hate to think of it.

These were years of fear and grieving at the Indian School, as many of Jerry's contemporaries and students were immersed in the world war, serving thousands of miles from home. Some, like Ben Quintana, did not survive. Juan's marked hearing loss kept him from serving in the forces, and so he and Jerry kept track of friends and students during those years.

At the conclusion of that school year of 1943, Jerry was in despair. A personality clash with another faculty member, whose antagonism toward her was not confined to their personal exchanges but bled into interactions with other faculty and students, left Jerry feeling isolated, hurt, and misjudged. Still, in May in a letter to Dunn, she indicated that something deep inside kept her at the school.

I almost quit this Spring but I don't know what keeps me here. . . . The last two years have been a misery. . . .

. . . We are not allowed to go to summer school unless it is at Haskell where they are having the Indian Service summer school so I guess I am going to have to stay here. I am not a bit interested in going there. Sister Henry from Rosary College is trying to help me to get in for their summer school and she is even trying to get them to cut down the expenses so I can get in but even at that I guess I will have to stay here. They are offering some good courses there and I surely would like to take [them]. I imagine I will get a lot out of the Art Institute where you studied, as it is so near Rosary.

Somehow, despite her ongoing differences with the administration, Jerry stayed on, and the Studio grew in reputation. In 1944, El Palacio again reviewed the school's May exhibit:

"The best exhibit in several years," is the verdict of the many enthusiastic visitors. . . . Of about 100 pictures, almost half were sold the first week. Prices ranged from fifty cents to twenty-five dollars. . . . The variety of subjects and ideas . . . indicates the excellence of the method of instruction, under the direction of Mrs. Geronima Cruz Montoya, graduate of the school from San Juan Pueblo. She has proven her ability by bringing up the quality of work this year against the great odds of having to start all over after almost all the artists trained under the former splendid teacher, Dorothy Dunn, had left for the armed forces. Mrs. Montoya's children who were beginners last year are now doing remarkably good work; and she has attained excellent results from the newer pupils this year. . . .

... Purchases have been made by the veteran collectors of the community; Bertha Dutton of the Museum staff, bought several; Mrs. C. H. Deitrich, chairman of the New Mexico Association on Indian Affairs, secured a number. Other purchases included Kenneth Chapman, of the Laboratory of Anthropology; Miss Mary Wheelwright of the Museum of Navajo Ceremonial Art. (*El Palacio*, May 1944, vol. 51, no. 5, 83–84)

The following year's exhibit also received high praise:

Approximately one hundred pictures represent the achievements of about twenty young artists who have worked under the guidance and direction of their teacher, Mrs. Juan Montoya, herself an Indian from San Juan pueblo . . . .

. . . The pictures . . . were well received . . . and a great many of them were sold during the two weeks they were displayed.

Mr. Alfred Morang, Santa Fe artist, who viewed the exhibit, believed that:

"The exhibition of paintings from the Indian School demonstrates that these Indian painters are approaching more and more closely the problems of both pictorial representation and abstraction with the tools provided by contemporary art. But there is no obvious imitation of existing methods; rather, the Indian artists are sensing the deeper emotional currents of our American life. . . .

"These papers seem invested with both racial and individual forces. The personality of the painters reaches through to the observer, but only because the painters succeed in projecting their emotional responses to their subject matter through an innate grasp of plastic design. . . .

". . . If there is any one lesson to be learned from this exhibition, it is that numerous painters represented here have found a union between their own native life and the movement of the civilization around them. Technically, most of the work is on a rather high plane, and emotionally, almost without exception, it occupies a place comparable with some of the best work being done by our American moderns." (*El Palacio*, 1945, vol. 52, no. 5, 81–82)

And yet again in 1948:

> Ten artists were represented in the group of tempera paintings from
> the Indian School. . . . Jeronima Montoya as painting teacher has
> helped bring into focus the attainment of the students during the
> year. Individual style is encouraged, as well as the traditional charac-
> ter of Indian painting, which is done simply, adhering to a heritage
> in pictorial expression which may have existed long before white
> men became aware of it around 1918. This two-dimensional work,
> with a strong suggestion of movement and rhythm, and excellent
> design and detail, has been compared to Persian, Japanese and
> Chinese work. The reason for encouraging the Indian's own style is
> that it has a beauty of its own—a dignity, poise, and quality of charm
> which strongly characterize the race and which no white artist can
> imitate." (*El Palacio*, June 1948, vol. 55, no. 6, 185)

Now almost a decade after she began as a young student teacher,
Jerry had well established her capacity to sustain the Studio and
nourish the talents of her students.

Three Sons

By 1941, Jerry and Juan's household in the small dormitory apartment
on the campus expanded to include Aunt Shine (Ramoncita) and
Stuka (Francis), Aunt Shine's infant son. Her husband, Gilbert, had
been sent for active combat on an aircraft carrier in the South Pacific.
Stuka won his nickname from his Uncle Juan in recognition of the
boy's efforts to imitate a dive bomber off the bed. When Stuka's
younger brother, Bill, arrived in 1943, the household expanded again.

During these first years of marriage and teaching, Jerry maintained constant and close contact with her sisters, all of whom,
except Adelaide, were living with growing families in Santa Fe. The
Montoyas saved their gas rationing coupons so they could drive to
San Juan to visit Pablo and Crucita, who delighted in watching
their grandchildren. Pablo and Crucita, Jerry and her sisters, and
some of the children would speak Téwa; the five sisters spoke English
with their husbands. A little Spanish sometimes bridged gaps.

(Top) *Indian School faculty, 1948. Jerry is eighth from the right and Juan third from the left. Family archives.* (Left) *The Cruz women on Queen's graduation from Santa Fe Indian School, 1940s. Left to right: Jerry, Piedad, Crucita, Pauline, Aunt Shine, Queen, Reycita, and Adelaide. Family archives.* (Right) *Family gathering for Pablo and Crucita Cruz's fiftieth wedding anniversary. Jerry is on the far left and Father Mueller on the far right. Family archives.*

In March 1947, Jerry gave birth to Robert; three years later, in 1950, to Paul; and in 1954, to Eugene. All were born at the Indian Hospital, and Jerry remembers that she was given three months off from teaching for each of their births. All were taken to San Juan to be named in Téwa by Jerry's mother. Crucita named her last three grandchildren carefully: Soê Khuwa P'in (Fog Mountain), Póvi Ta' (Marked Flower), and P'oesay (Dew). Catholic baptism took place at St. Francis Cathedral in Santa Fe, in the presence of the god-parents: "Tony [García] and Pie. . . . That was our custom in San Juan: that you select a godparent for the first one and then they carry on and if one of them dies, then you can change godparents."

Juan was always active in the boys' upbringing and care from the time they were infants. "[Juan] was a very caring person. Real helpful in the home. He helped with the babies. When they were babies he would get up and . . . helped with the 2 A.M. feeding and I changed the diapers. . . . Or [with] the milk and stuff like that."

Just as Jerry and Juan had been able to help Aunt Shine when Gilbert was away, now Aunt Shine and Gilbert were able to take care of Robert, Paul, and Eugene as well as their own two older boys, Stuka and Bill. Both families now shared a larger house on the Indian School campus. Aunt Shine stayed home with the boys while her husband went to his job as a plasterer and the Montoyas walked across campus to their classrooms. Often, Aunt Shine took care of the boys in the evenings and on weekends, too:

> I was baby sitting. . . . Well, we just moved in with them and we had Stuka and Bill—they were much older than Bobby. So we moved in with Juan and Jerry, I was keeping house. I wasn't working.
>
> Bill [Piedad's husband] had already died. . . . She was the dieti-cian at the [Indian] Hospital [and living] at the nurses' residence. For a while, she stayed with us too.

The families are very close—best companions and playmates. Jerry remembers many family outings together, as does Aunt Shine: "After work we used to go fishing by the Tesuque River. Just take a picnic lunch and then they would fish. The boys did a lot of fish-ing, especially Gene and Bobby. That's what they enjoyed when they were small."

With the leadership of Juan and Father Joel from San Juan Pueblo, the families also established a baseball team for the young boys at San Juan, even before their own sons were old enough to play on it. Aunt Shine and Jerry recall this time together:

(Left) *Pablo and Crucita Cruz on their fiftieth wedding anniversary. Family archives.* (Right) *Jerry and Juan with their three sons in their home at the Indian School, c.1955). Left to right: Juan, Robert, Paul, Eugene, and Jerry. Family archives.*

Jerry: We used to spend a lot of time at baseball games. Juan was the manager of the Hawks team. The family spent weekend after weekend making popcorn and—

Aunt Shine: Selling pop.

Jerry: Yeah, and selling to benefit the team. Juan [started the team]—Juan and Father—

Aunt Shine: —Joel. We started it to keep them out of mischief.

Jerry: Something to look forward to doing. So we spent our weekends at baseball games. I guess we were in San Juan every weekend at that time. They had Indian league both in the northern and southern pueblos. So we traveled from place to place every weekend. We were at one game or another.

Aunt Shine: We used to take the boys—some of the team.

Jerry: And [Juan] went to San Juan to practice with the boys. I think he felt closer to the boys here at San Juan [than in his pueblo]. And [our] boys were [living] closer to San Juan than to Sandia. It was a family affair [laughs]. Well, our boys, they were just babies. They grew up in baseball. None of them were big enough to be playing at the time. They hung around the team. The ball players were very good to my sons.

Jerry still has an award given to Juan "in grateful appreciation" for his work as "manager of the San Juan Hawks for years of dedicated service to the team he led to the Pennant and Championship of the All Indian Baseball League, 1959."

"He Touched the Hearts and Souls of Many."

Robert, now in his forties, writes of his father with great love:

"Is your father Juan Montoya?" This question I have answered so proudly time and time again, "Yes!" A phenomenal reputation established by both my father and my mother preceded all of us as we began our professions here in New Mexico.

Known as father, husband, uncle, brother-in-law, grandfather, godfather, leader, and chieftain, my father was, without a doubt, the most influential male figure in my life. He touched the hearts and souls of many people, Indian and non-Indian. He truly demonstrated that his fairness and his ability to lead made him the person so respected. . . .

My father was truly an individual of wisdom enhanced by his ability to learn from experiences of his life and the life of others. He was a person wise in Indian culture and tradition, a person known for his ability to render wise and fair decisions over personal or cultural controversies. Looking to the future was my father's keenest sense and guide, always prepared with anticipation, quick to act if necessary and always seeking alternatives.

As Jerry remembers:

[Juan] was a good dad. His profession was a carpenter. Then as the years went by, he became head of maintenance over there at the Indian School.

[*] [Juan] preferred doing the manual work himself. [*] I think he knew every basement in that school there. All the pipes. He fell one time in one of the basements and he hurt his ankle and I was telling him to report to the supervisor and let them pay for the insurance or whatever. But he didn't listen. He had problems with his ankle after that. I think they had a leak somewhere and he was trying to locate the leak.

Juan Montoya in his carpenter's shop at the Santa Fe Indian School, 1950s. Family archives.

[*] He made frames, tables, and furniture, and stuff like that—just for [us]. [*] He made an altar for Sandia. He enjoyed carpentry.

Then he started carving birds. I still have one that he carved and never got to paint. But it is beautiful in just the natural wood without having it painted.

Juan was president of the alumni association for years too. When we went to see Pula's wife, to offer our condolences after Pula passed away, while we were visiting in there, this girl came out with a letter and said "Look what I found in the bathroom!" and there was a letter from Juan to Pula inviting him to the homecoming [laughs]. [*] We were so surprised!

Juan taught our boys the Indian culture, the ceremonies, our Indian way—and Ron [great-nephew] was telling Paul that his father [Sam Arquero] made a remark to him: he said, "Look what the boys are doing. Look what Juan taught them. They are carrying on the things they learned."

Juan was well loved at the Indian School, too, so well loved that in April 1985 a hall at the school was named after him. The dedication stated:

> Characterized by patient caring, persistence, and known by his family and friends as a steady person who spoke in a kind way, he gave a lifetime to the Santa Fe Indian School.
>
> Born in Sandia Pueblo on September 20, 1913, Juan entered the Santa Fe Indian School in 1918 at the young age of five. He spent all of his school years at SFIS, graduating in 1937.
>
> Beginning as a school carpenter in 1939, Juan became an instructor in carpentry and cabinet making in 1946, teaching students the art of his Trade from 1949–1952. He worked again as a carpenter in 1952. Juan became a general building repair man. He knew his small school inside and out. His employment tenure continued through his retirement in 1973 on June 29.
>
> Juan Montoya Hall, housing the youngest of our children, stands as a special tribute to a very special man.

When Jerry and Aunt Shine are asked if they have some favorite stories about Juan, especially about his capacity to tease, they reply:

> Jerry: Maybe she does [laughs, pointing]! Somebody asked me that just the other day, if Juan was like the boys. He joked a lot. He gave everyone, I think, a nickname. That's what he was famous for. Every one of our kids and all of the other nieces and nephews, they all have nicknames. Stuka—
>
> Aunt Shine: He didn't have nicknames for [his sons] but he had nicknames for—
>
> Jerry: Erin was "Irinaya," Frankie was—what was Frankie?
>
> Aunt Shine: He was just born, remember, when he [Juan] died.
>
> Jerry: Oh, he didn't get to know Frankie.
>
> Aunt Shine: Also Glenda—
>
> Jerry: Yeah, Glenda was "Blender." Ethel is "LuLu" and Evelyn is "Ev" and "F.I."
>
> Aunt Shine: María is "María Tortilla."
>
> Jerry: Yes, "María Tortilla." He had a nickname for Eddie:

Eduardo—and "Rodríguez"! He had nicknames for all of them [laughs].

When asked what makes a good Pueblo marriage and the sorts of values she considers important, Jerry reflects:

> I think it is understanding and trusting. The relatives talk to the bride and the groom and give them advice. Advice after advice but—I think we have to know that there is a Supreme Being that is above everyone else. There is a God that we trust that we ask for help. I think if they have that religion, you know, and have faith, I think their marriage would work. I think they will understand. But so many now just don't seem to care.
>
> [In marriage] you are one. That's the Pueblo—and the Catholic— belief. And Steven Trujillo [a Pueblo elder] said our Pueblo religion and our Catholic religion are the same. We honor the same God. So relatives speak to the couple and advise that they are married for life. They should not listen to gossip. They have to be trusting. They always tell the ladies that when your husband comes home, have a meal ready for him. That is one thing they were always telling the bride. Be waiting for your husband and have meals ready for him. They still do that. Just recently it was the fiftieth anniversary of our cousin. The fiftieth wedding anniversary. So you don't hear of divorces among the older people.

"School Took Forever!"

While she was teaching, Jerry continued to study. In 1942, she took evening classes in shorthand and typing. During the summers of 1947 and 1948, she traveled to Claremont, California, to study with Alfredo Ramos Martínez, the renowned Mexican muralist and painter, and Jean Ames of Claremont College, whose sense of design was influential in Jerry's later paintings. Juan drove Aunt Shine, Jerry, and their two eldest boys, Stuka and Robert, across the desert and then back again to pick them up at the end of the summers. Apart from a near tragedy, when Stuka saved his younger cousin from drowning in a pool, the time in California was joyful.

Jerry on the campus of Scripps College, where she took courses with Jean Ames and Alfredo Martínez, 1948. Family archives.

I learned design qualities from [Jean Ames]. She was very important in helping get ideas going. She used to give different projects for different days. I used my Indian ideas but she was good at helping me put different idioms, as she called it, together. [*] I took courses with [Mexican muralist Alfredo Martínez] at Scripps in 1947 and 1948. He was one of the finest teachers I ever had.

Virginia Clark Bailey was my roommate when I began teaching at the Indian School. She was the music teacher. She could have been Indian, she understood so much without asking. My first trip to California was with her in 1937, when we stayed with her folks.

I saw the Pacific Ocean for the first time then, and they took me to swim in it. The beach was so white, and the water and waves looked nice and warm, but I nearly froze when I went in!

Later, I stayed with the Bailey family again when I went to the Claremont College to study.

Nights, Saturdays, and summers were regular school days for Jerry. She had started part-time study for her bachelor of science degree at St. Joseph's College, later to become the University of Albuquerque.

> We knew that sooner or later the school was going to be accredited and that we would need degrees. When the school became accredited we had to have our teacher's certificate to teach. Since I started teaching after I graduated from high school, I didn't go to college so I had to start taking courses—and of course I was interested in learning more anyway. We had to earn so many hours during the summer in order to renew our teaching certificates. So I thought I could start slowly. I'm not such a brilliant person—I have to work hard. I got my degree; I earned it bit by bit—just through summer school and night classes.
>
> [*] People accepted my doing the studying but I guess they thought it was—unusual. Juan, I guess, was pretty unusual. He helped at the house. The other kids would say "I wish my Daddy would do that." And he did cooking when I wasn't there. He'd fix what he called "Bachelor's Delight"—stew! He helped with cooking and housework. . . . And then he would wash dishes, help with the dishes. [*] Helped raise the boys.

Jerry's major was art; her minor, education. She loved learning. The art classes, however, being strictly Western in orientation, were a challenge at times: "I hated having to go out and sketch old houses and still lifes and models. It seemed more like copying. I guess I was being a 'stubborn Indian' about being made to observe."

As part of her degree Jerry took classes in elementary school teaching (education, methods in science, intermediate reading and arithmetic, special methods in social studies, physical science, art, and health education), secondary methods and techniques, and audiovisual aids. She also studied educational philosophy, psychology, and the pedagogy of apologetics.

> School took forever! There was St. Joseph's and then the BIA had summer sessions for teachers. I went to night classes, Saturday classes, summer classes, just whenever I could get in.
>
> My husband was so good with the kids. They'd take me down and

if anything was going on in Sandia they would stop and spend the day with the folks. And they loved to go up to the petroglyphs or to West Mesa, or just go on into Albuquerque and watch the Albuquerque Civic Auditorium being built while I went to class. I received my degree the hard way.

Finally, in 1958, she was awarded her bachelor of science degree from St. Joseph's College in Albuquerque.

"We Knew the Boys Would Need Real Fine Teachers."

When the time came for each of the three boys to go to school, Jerry and Juan faced a difficult decision. The Santa Fe Indian School was not open to children of SFIS employees.

Juan and I had found out how important education is. We knew the boys would need real fine teachers to make their way in the world. We finally decided to send them to parochial and private school. They went to St. Francis Parochial School first, then on to St. Michael's High School. It cost students twenty-five dollars a month to go to St. Michael's. It was run by the Christian Brothers.

When it was time for Gene to go to St. Francis, we had bought our own house and it was in a different parish, so he couldn't attend St. Francis, so he went to live with Mother in San Juan for a year and attended parochial school there. That was where he came to understand Téwa, even though he never spoke it. The other boys never learned because Juan and I can't understand each other's language, so we always communicated in English.

Their decision about their boys' education was well-founded. Robert graduated from the University of New Mexico and won a fellowship to attend the master's program in regional and city planning from the University of Oklahoma. Paul became a criminal investigator with the BIA Police and is police chief in Laguna. Eugene went on to take a bachelor of arts degree in social work and business at New Mexico State and became a juvenile probation officer with the State.

"I'll Do My Best with My Few."

During these years of study and raising her sons, Jerry's devotion to the Studio and its vision stayed firm, if embattled. By 1954, the year her third son, Eugene, was born, she had only a few students in the Studio, which she found discouraging. She also felt the pressures of outside forces calling for Indians to become "white collar workers" and how these turned the students toward commercial fields. She felt that this was a sad waste of talent. She also was less and less in a position to send out exhibit notices, this now being the purview of the Arts and Crafts Department. She commented to Dunn: "Oh well, I'll do my best with my few. I am hoping to do a couple of paintings to send to De Young Gallery in San Francisco. I certainly hope to find some time—I don't know when."

Dunn replied in a lengthy, typewritten letter that gives glimpses of her continuing commitment to the development of Indian art, her ongoing interest in the school, her strong role as a mentor for Jerry, and her deep affection for and friendship with Jerry and her family.

> On my last trip to Santa Fe to get the exhibit ready to ship, I though[t] sure I would get to see you at the studio and go over your work with you. I had wanted to for a long time. But I found the time taken up with rounding paintings from over town, measuring mats, erasing marks off some dirty mats, typing lists, giving a radio and newspaper interview scheduled for me by Hester but not planned on by me, etc. etc. . . .
>
> When I saw your paintings at the [Gallup] Ceremonial this year, I was happy to see that you were finding time, with both a job and a family, to do some work of your own. And very good work, too. I remember I put a blue ribbon on one of your paintings. The little miniatures are especially lovely, I think. And I saw one at Mrs. [collector Lianne] Adam's—above her sink, I think, of a bird that was the best of all. I think you could carry this miniature painting a long way if your eyes can stand it.
>
> I am sorry to hear you that you have so few students. No other career they could train for would be better than painting—for those

114 ▪ *The Talent That Was There*

(LEFT) *Jerry, outside the Studio, Santa Fe Indian School, about 1940. Family archives.* (RIGHT) *Jerry showing a student how to silk-screen in the Studio in the late 1950s. Family archives.*

that have real talent and want to paint, I mean. The market is opening wider and wider all the time. I get letters from everywhere saying, "Where can I buy Indian paintings?" and I don't know where to send them or tell them to write where they can always find a supply of good ones.

You ask about paintings murals at the studio. I would not recommend any sort of ceremonial things for the porch, if you do decide to paint there. Perhaps smaller units of abstract design such as [are] found on pottery or in sandpaintings would go there—nothing very realistic with the simple, geometric lines of the building. Where murals were badly needed, and perhaps still are, is the upper wall of the studio itself. I remember how ashamed I was when visitors would look up at those scattered, partly finished things and think those were our murals. . . . I would paint out the old beginnings and make fresh murals—a procession from beginning to end all around the room. Tell the painters to work for "happy things," to get as much joy and gaiety in paintings as possible—burlesques, games, mudhead pranks, gay birds and other animals. The space is not high, so murals will be small and could be quite bright in color. These murals should give one a "lift" when he sees them, nothing sombre, sad, or dull. What do you think?

By the way, do you know whatever happened to those big murals made on canvas and masonite by the older artists under Olive's direction? I would like to have photographs made of them but no-one seems to know what became of them.

It will be one year on the 4th since Mom died, and I cannot think it has been so long. . . . Right now I look around the room and see so many things to remind me of her—a plant she started, a basket Pablita [Velarde] gave her, and the grinding sticks you gave her, among other things. She meant a lot to many people. She was always calm and peaceful, much like an Indian woman of the Pueblos, now that I come to think of it. Maybe that is why they understood and loved her. She always inquired about all of you whom she knew, and spoke often and lovingly of each one. I am grateful to you for writing her and sending pictures of the children. These meant a lot to her, and she cared for everything to the end. . . .

I wish you could come some time and I could show you these and other things of Mom's; also some of her pictures. Some longer holiday, like Thanksgiving or vacation, maybe you and Juan and the boys can plan a Juarez [Mexico] trip and stop with us going and coming. We have room to sleep you all and would love to have you visit. . . .

We all hope you and your family will have a happy Christmas and we are sure you will. . . .

I hope all your folks are well. I remember the beautiful rose-tan bowl your mother made for me which was broken in the move to Las Cruces along with some other pottery that I valued highly. But I remember just how it looked and will always.

With love to all of you. (letter provided by Dunn)

Things were still not easy around the Studio, however, a fact to which Dunn alludes in a letter to Jerry in late January 1959. It is clear from Dunn's responses that Jerry was encountering difficulties; she appeared to be finding it almost impossible to provide what

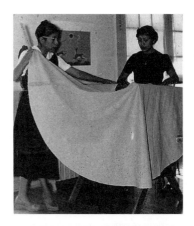

(LEFT) *Jerry helping a young student with design work in the Studio in the late 1950s. Family archives.* (RIGHT) *Jerry and other officers of the Indian School Alumni Association, making plans for homecoming. Left to right: Mike Harrier, President; Trinidad Perez, Vice-President; Jerry, Secretary Treasurer. Family archives.* (BELOW) *Meeting at the Indian School, late 1950s. Left to right: Piedad Antoine, Faustin Talachy, Gladys Perez, Joe Sando, Jerry, Gilbert Sandoval , Reycita, and Ramoncita. Family archives.*

she considered minimal learning and creative experimentation for her students under the scheduling constraints of short periods and one twelve-week class alone.

From several sources—and some very high—outside the Education Office of Indian Affairs, I have heard rumblings of dissatisfaction with the way things are going with the Arts and Crafts all over the Indian Service. I don't know what steps the Arts and Crafts Board is taking, or if it can fight the Indian policies in the Indian Office, but I do know for a fact that the Ford and Rockefeller Foundations have at last awakened to the importance of Indian Art and have already granted funds for inquiries into the whole subject. I know because I have been asked to furnish information for both foundations. Some good is bound to come out of it in time, so hang on and grit your teeth. Do the best you can with what you have.

Lesson plans are ridiculous anywhere and especially for art teaching. But if they are required, spend as little time on them as possible and remember you don't have to follow thematically. You've just got to use creativity and spur-of-the-moment judgment every hour of such a job. So much cannot be predicted or planned. Most of the best things are surprises to both artist and teacher, as you well know.

It is hard to give suggestions on your classes unless I know what age groups they are. . . . Are most of them beginners? Can any of them return for more work later this school year, or is the twelve week period all? Is painting elective or required? How big are the classes? Does 45 minutes cover time for changing from class to class? If so, you don't have them much over a half hour and that of course must cover getting and putting away materials. Well, I see what you're up against! Are students allowed to come in freely on their own time in evenings and Saturdays as they did when I was there? . . .

I saw some very fine work at Gallup last August from your class, the best I've seen in years. . . . Things from Alb. were poor and very few. Only you and Fred Kabotie's Oraibi High sent in work that was going places—and one or two little things from Jemez. It is no less than a crime if such work has to be cut off by ignorant [illegible].

. . . I'll give you whatever advice I think may work over this long distance, and I'll know better what to report to the Ford and Rockefeller inquiries. . . .

In the meantime, spend some time on color mixing and application—at least the first week for each new class. I don't see how you can take any time for the sort of schematic drawings we used to do to help them begin to loosen up; you'll just have to sail into pictures as soon as possible. I would encourage more small pictures especially at first so they can see they are finishing something—single figures, single animals, single abstract motifs etc. Then small groups. Many students may never get beyond these smaller pictures but some may be very nice. You can help decide whom to encourage to undertake more elaborate paintings, and lead into bigger works for more and more students who want to do them in the latter part of the 12 week period. (letter provided by Dunn)

Jerry was presumably encouraged to continue for a while longer doing what she could in a situation that was, for her, increasingly confining and counter-creative. To the end of her years at the school, she attempted to consolidate and expand upon Dorothy Dunn's vision. In 1962 the tide, however, was turning against their artistic and teaching philosophies. It would be another thirty years before Jerry would be recognized once again, in the nineties, as one of the major contributors to the uniquely influential and culturally profound American Indian art movement.

5
NO PLACE FOR US
The Closing of the Studio

Loyalty and Loss

Jerry's commitment to family, ceremonial life, and teaching were immutable, as was her loyalty to the artistic perspective held by Dorothy Dunn and Kenneth Chapman and adapted by Jerry in her quarter of a century of teaching. Daily life, with its exigencies, stresses, joys, and achievements, was mutable.

What she held immutable would become the basis for her alienation from the art-teaching world she had helped to create; it also would give her unshakable clarity, strength, and integrity in an impossible situation. What she held mutable would sustain her philosophically and practically over the period of greatest loss she had experienced in her life: the death of her teaching in the form it had always taken, followed closely by the deaths of two family members.

Hers was—and is—an essentially feminine and Pueblo response to crisis. Knowing she could not change her aesthetic values, she protested callous and demeaning professional treatment by an incoming administration. Yet in no way did she view her actions as heroic. She knew her approach would result eventually in her ousting, but she accepted this outcome with neither a sense of victimization (although certainly that was inherent in the political situation) nor of failure. Her acceptance carried her through with a strength that came not from power but from spiritual pragmatism.

Gathering Forces

The early sixties ushered in an era of Pan-Indian self-determination that evoked strong feelings and often militant actions throughout the country. Under the pressure of factors such as this, national conceptions of Indian art were changing dramatically.

> The origins of contemporary Indian easel painting have been traced to Plains ledger drawings . . . and to Southwestern drawings and paintings encouraged by anthropologists and school art teachers. . . . The themes of these were greatly influenced by the interests of those for whom they were drawn. Aside from the themes, there are unresolved problems over the sources of the styles: how much they are "native," "aboriginal," "traditional," or even, according to some naive commentators (including some teachers and some of their Indian students), innate. How much is style influenced by art teachers and other non-Indian consumers and the models they provided? . . . [Indian artists] participated in a school of painting that changed and developed (and ultimately stultified) through formal teaching and by informal imitation, reacting to the standards of a body of consumers that included teachers, jurors of shows, curators, collectors—and other Indian artists, but rarely or never other non-artist members of Indian communities (although there are some well-known instances of negative sanctions applied to artists by Pueblo communities). (Sturtevant, in Wade 1986, 38)

Robert A. Ewing, curator-in-charge of the Fine Arts Division, Museum of New Mexico, succinctly expressed the attitude toward "traditional Indian art" that began to prevail in the summer of 1961 and has divided artists and critics ever since. (See *El Palacio,* Spring 1969, vol. 76, no. 1, 33–39.) Ewing was unapologetically in favor of the "new Indian art." His story of what happened during those turbulent years of 1961 and 1962 lends counterpoint to Jerry's experience. At first he praises the Studio work: "The highly designed, flat tempera paintings which became accepted as most representative of American Indian art were original and exciting, and in their design and content were the obvious continuation of a great art heritage." However, his comments quickly become strongly ambivalent. Within the paragraph in which he calls the early work "beautifully imaginative," he describes the same artists as restricted, stereotypical, childlike, and unchallenging to the intellect. Most condemnatory is his discussion of the teaching style that he sees as nothing less than dictatorial:

> Well meaning teachers guided young Indian artists into what had become the "official" style without regard to their natural tendencies and abilities. As a result, a group of American artists was as restricted in choice of style and technique as if it had existed in a totalitarian society. If a young Indian artist wished to exhibit and sell his work, he soon learned to adopt the popular "Indian" style. . . .
>
> Despite the best of intentions, a patronizing attitude toward Indian art could not be avoided. Indian paintings were charming and childlike, and the Indian artist was not expected to challenge the intellect. He was simply to delight the viewer. It must not be forgotten that many of the early painters in this style produced beautifully imaginative works of art which rank with the best art production of any age. But inevitably, much of Indian art fell into a static repetition of the accepted, and easily recognized, style.

Ewing sees the turning point against conformity in Indian art to be the experience of World War II and its chaotic aftermath that exposed so many young Indian men to unfamiliar and sophisticated cultures and European art styles and materials. He then includes an encomium for Lloyd Kiva New—whose antipathy toward Dorothy Dunn and the Studio style was by then established gossip, calling him one of the "most gifted of these young creators" participating in the Rockefeller Project.

> The Rockefeller Project was an experimental probe of the thesis that Indian sources and traditions could be combined with contemporary idioms and techniques. The project was held at the University of

Arizona at Tucson during the summers of 1961 and 1962 and consisted of a series of lectures, seminars and workshops with studios provided for the actual production of works of art.

New, later director and now President Emeritus of the IAIA [Institute of American Indian Arts], headed the project. A number of talented Indians attended the seminars and participated in such experiments as going out to the Navajo Reservation to sketch from life and returning to the studio environment to develop these sketches into designs for fabric, jewelry, pottery and painting.

Ewing highlights indirectly an important philosophical shift that took place at this time: the shift in focus from "American Indian art" to "American Indian artists." The new school's position was that any art done by an American Indian was American Indian art, regardless of style or break with tradition.

> A unique government institution, the Institute has brought together
> . . . dedicated instructors to work with an extremely heterogeneous
> group of creative young people who share only the common bond of
> being American Indians. All of the students at the IAIA make a thor-
> ough study of the rich and enormously varied traditions of Indian
> America. World art is studied and the students participate in a range
> of creative experiences utilizing the skills of teachers who work in the
> wide variety of contemporary media. . . . So each student is treated as
> an individual. . . . There is no uniform approach to the creative act.

Ewing's last comment about the lack of uniformity ignores, however, the rapidly growing uniformity within the rebellion that characterized IAIA. If the Studio evidenced convergent thinking among its students, so did IAIA. While artists such as T. C. Cannon and Fritz Scholder were breaking artistic ground, many students were painting in the styles of Scholder and Cannon, no matter how their teachers encouraged originality.

This tendency toward convergent thinking raises issues about the role of group influence and consensus even in a new and fluid situation. A cursory glance at the cultural mores of American Indian people shows that, in most groups, communal values take precedence over individualism—particularly among Pueblo peoples. Teaching of crafts in the Pueblo communities happens by cultural osmosis. While young potters are encouraged to develop their pottery any way they like, most gravitate toward collectively inspired styles, as do embroiderers, basket makers, and jewelry makers. Is it surprising then, that each group of students—at the Studio and at IAIA—learned from their particular elders and from each other, each group thus creating a style, a precedent, which then became a desirable source of inspiration? Perhaps their own sense of interconnectedness with and openness to each other was even stronger than anything Dorothy Dunn, Jerry Montoya, Lloyd Kiva New, T. C. Cannon, or Fritz Scholder had to teach them.

In contrast to many retrospective perceptions, many Indian people, particularly older ones, actually believed that certain young and ambitious artists wanted this new Institute as a showcase for their own work and that they had maneuvered the change to do this. Since the art work from the old boarding school had been of the highest order during Jerry's tenure, this was a natural place for an art school to be launched.

According to Jamake Highwater, author of several books on American Indians:

> Institutional acceptance of modernist trends in Indian art did not blossom suddenly at the IAIA, however; it had a quiet but long-standing underground existence in the art community. For instance, in an interview with Jeanne Snodgrass, Indian arts curator from 1956 to 1969 at Philbrook Art Center, I was told: "In 1959, three years prior to the opening of the Institute, Philbrook Art Center presented paintings generally considered to be taking a new direction. Thus Philbrook provided the first major endorsement of the evolution in Indian art and acknowledged the ever-increasing desire of artists to experiment—not to break from their culture, but to explore it and improvise upon it—to effect an integration with the demands of the present. . . . The new direction treatment, first accepted by the Philbrook, later by more recent annual exhibitions, and certainly encouraged by the IAIA, is but one more phase in the continuous development of Indian art." (Highwater, in Wade 1986, 237)

The Indian School Changeover

In 1960, for a national juried exhibit at the Museum of New Mexico Art Gallery, Jerry wrote a foreword that indirectly addresses the growing perception of her philosophy as restrictive and out of touch with national and international trends and interest:

> These annual American Indian painting exhibitions have encouraged many young Indian artists. They have realized that they have something wonderful and unique to contribute to the art world. . . . They have also found that fine Indian art is in demand throughout the nation.
>
> Art lovers throughout the United States, especially in Santa Fe, have done much to encourage and promote the Indian Art movement. It is because of this encouragement that the Santa Fe Indian School Arts and Crafts program is now being reactivated. This program will be in full swing beginning with the fall term. Indian students from all over the United States and Alaska who meet the criteria for enrollment will be accepted. . . .
>
> In this show one will find traditional Indian painting as well as modern contemporary art. They are modern in style yet ancient in symbolism—which is part of the daily life of an Indian.

Her private feelings about the Studio were less optimistic. In the spring of 1961, Jerry was feeling increasingly confined and isolated. She feared that her continuing to teach what she referred to simply as "Indian art" would result in her being fired. Eventually, it happened. According to Jerry's records, administrative emphasis and teacher assessment at this time focused increasingly on the correct completion of operational guide sheets and curricula forms. The spontaneity and intuitive freedom she valued so much as ideals for her classes were drowning in a flood of educational goals, lesson plans, and restricted activities. She discussed these concerns with Dunn in private and in a letter voiced her commitment to nourish her own creativity by sending out paintings:

> I have enough paintings to send to the Smith College Club. I got

real busy in February and painted a few small ones and some medium size ones. I thought about sending some to Philbrook but instead I will let the Smith College Club show them. You tell the president that I will get them to her in plenty of time. Let me know what you think about them when you see them. I want you to be my critic. (93 DDK)

"I Was Alone in There."

In 1962, the Santa Fe Indian School was terminated by the government and replaced by the Institute of American Indian Arts, envisioned originally by the Eisenhower administration as an arts and crafts college for nationwide intertribal high school and post-graduate students. The decision to close the school was made by the federal government without consulting the SFIS students or staff or Pueblo leaders. SFIS students were forced to go to the Albuquerque Indian School or to local public schools, which were not prepared for Indian students. The Institute was to be an art school with a philosophy radically different from the Studio's—one with which Jerry Montoya's approach did not conform:

> They kept saying we were doing the same thing over and over again, that it was a stereotype of work and that we didn't do any creative work. Now Dorothy never told us we had to do it a certain way. She always encouraged us to be creative. But that's the way they thought about our work. They always argued: "But as long as it's done by an Indian, it's Indian art!"

At the time of the changeover, the forcible reassignment of many faculty who had influenced the lives of hundreds of young Indians resulted in a nearly complete turnover of teachers. Mary Mitchell, head of the Indian School art department at the time, recommended to Jerry that she attend the Rockefeller Project summer classes at the University of Arizona in 1960 and 1961.

> Lloyd New was the teacher at that time when we were there. We would meet in the evenings and discuss how to change. By then, all

they wanted was to change the way that we were doing [things]. I think they were already planning the changeover.

Well, I am very much of a traditionalist so I continued to encourage our traditional way of painting. I think Mr. Chapman said it the best at one of the classes that I attended. He said that our Indian art is ancient as well as modern. . . . He said that what is being done now is just a fad: it lives for a day and then changes.

No-one else agreed with me—I was alone in there. But I didn't feel bad. I always sensed what they were trying to do. I just didn't worry about it.

Jerry encountered opposition not only at the summer school, but also daily when she returned to SFIS to teach. Criticism of teachers who belonged to the earlier wave was heavy; teachers were criticized for not having correct curricula, for not following orders. The atmosphere was antagonistic and fearful; morale among faculty was low.

We knew that none of us had a chance to stay on because when the announcements came out—you know, the bulletins describing the positions—I went down the line and I said, "Now this is for Alan Houser; this is for Charles Loloma; this is for Otellie Loloma. . . ." And all down the line that is exactly the way it came up. The job descriptions fit certain people and they are the ones that got the jobs.

The new teachers came down right after IAIA took over. They took over the art buildings and we were teaching out of one of the dorm rooms. I was upstairs in what was then called Crandall Hall. They switched us. I was supposed to be fired; they just said that I needn't apply for a job. But instead, they gave me elementary kids—fifth and sixth graders, I think.

The Studio ended as it began. Just as Dorothy Dunn had agreed to take on the job of fifth grade teacher in order to create a way to found the Studio, so now, as the Studio was closed, Jerry was forced to accept a position as fifth grade teacher in order to stay on.

The position of the new administration was later made clear

by Lloyd Kiva New, director of the new IAIA from 1967 to 1980: "I don't think these decisions about what Indians should do in capturing the beauties of their rich past in contemporary dramatic forms should be made by [older] people" (Highwater, in Wade 1986, 238).

By strange coincidence, the Museum of New Mexico, Santa Fe, opened an exhibit that was called, in a review in the *New Mexican*, "probably the definitive collection of modern American Indian art." The collection was Margretta Dietrich's. According to the article, Dietrich's personal collection included paintings from 1921 to 1957, a period Dietrich called—rather pointedly it would seem—the "golden age" of modern Indian painting. The article elaborates:

> It was then that many of the founding artists, still in their prime, were augmented by hundreds of Indian youths who had begun to paint for the first time. Much of this new Indian enthusiasm for painting is laid to Mrs. Dietrich's efforts at encouraging youngsters to paint and at her insistence that they maintain the high standards of workmanship and the integrity shown by their predecessors. (Sunday, Nov. 11, 1962)

Struggling for Reassignment

For Jerry and Juan, the spring of 1962 was a nightmare. They attended one meeting after another—first with the department heads at the school, then with the chief personnel officer of the BIA United Pueblos Agency in the Gallup area, and finally with a member of the Civil Service Commission from Denver—in an effort to find employment after being "reassigned." Neither Jerry nor Juan had taken the Civil Service examination. They were, after all, working for the BIA and had "preferred status" as Indians teaching Indians. Had they taken that examination, they would have had the right to reinstatement in an available job for which they qualified, and without competition from the public.

The Denver Civil Service Commission member agreed that the Santa Fe Indian School employees were in a hard spot, but he told them this sort of thing happened constantly in military and forestry services. "I deal with it all the time even in the Civil Service Commission," Jerry remembers he told them. To its credit, the Commission did attempt to reassign all of the employees rather than resort to what they called a "reduction in force."

The Commission sent all reassigned employees a memorandum listing fourteen vacant positions for which they might apply. These were of little help to Jerry. None of them was in Santa Fe: Cañoncito, Albuquerque, Magdalena, Taos, and Santo Domingo Pueblo. Also, there was nothing on the list even remotely related to Jerry's training; the best jobs were teaching home economics, chemistry, music, and mathematics or working as a clerk-typist.

The Montoyas faced even further complications in that they both worked in the same school. While the new Institute retained Juan no longer as a teacher but as director of maintenance and grounds, it did not retain Jerry as an art teacher. Although Jerry qualified in every way for the appointment she had held, the new superintendent, Dr. George A. Boyce, wanted fewer traditional artists in the new institution and told Jerry, as he told all of the arts and crafts staff, that "he had no place for us in his Institute."

In Jerry's draft of one of many applications and appeals she made at this time, she analyzed her qualifications for the position. In order to become department head of fine arts at the new IAIA, she was expected to have "three years experience or training in a trade, craft, occupation, or subject appropriate to this position." Jerry pointed out that she had a bachelor of science degree, with a major in art and a minor in education.

The position required someone with "sufficient knowledge and ability to demonstrate, explain, and instruct students in the use of tools, techniques, principles; [and] three years in teaching or instructing in an adult education program, secondary school, college or industrial establishment." Jerry replied that she had "27 years in the Indian Service [as a] teacher [of] Arts and Crafts at the Santa Fe Indian School" and that she was Indian herself.

Last, the position required that an applicant be "an accomplished worker in the fields of a variety of media; [and] professionally recognized in his field of art." Despite her habit of and belief in modesty, Jerry managed to say that she believed that she was, by now, "professionally recognized as an artist and as an educator," as evidenced by a "School of American Research Purchase Award in Santa Fe." She noted that she had received a "special category prize in Gallup [and a] Scottsdale special category prize" and was listed in *Who's Who in American Art, Who's Who in the West,* and *Who's Who in New Mexico.* She added a parenthesis: "There are other awards but the above are recent."

The personal data that she supplied—apparently expected in any kind of application or appeal process—included her concerns about taking her boys, then eight, twelve, and fifteen, out of "good private schools," not wanting to be separated from Juan who had been tentatively assigned to the Institute, and wishing to keep the same doctor under whose care she had been for the past year. The Montoyas also had, by this time, bought a home in Santa Fe on the south side and were reluctant to leave, having taken, like many couples, years to establish themselves financially.

Yet, no matter how qualified Jerry was for the position, she was not welcome at the new Institute. More welcome was one of her students, whose career was flourishing: Henry Gobin, the Snohomish boy Jerry had guided not only in his art work, but also in becoming acquainted with his own cultural background. As recently as 1961, in fact, Jerry had encouraged Gobin to enter his painting in a competition in which it took first prize and subsequently appeared on the cover of the June 1962 issue of *New Mexico Wildlife.* Now this man was to become, for a time, the head of the fine arts department.

"They Should Have Kept the School." (Student, Indian School)

The school year ended with no resolution to the Montoya's problems. The principal and staff wrote a poignant two-page farewell letter to the departing students, acknowledging their sadness at the school's closing, ongoing concern for each student's welfare and success, and offering guidance on ways to adapt to a new school and to live a full life. In closing, it reminded the students of the school's ideals as written in the official handbook:

Make your record one that you can be proud of, proud because it shows your good progress and how you have overcome weaknesses and mistakes. Have high ideals, keep your ideals, and try to live by them in order to become the fine person you can and should be.

The closing was marked by Florence Ann Beasley, acting agency director of schools for the United Pueblos Agency, in a June 7 memorandum:

On May 10, 1962, the great educational institution of Santa Fe Indian School ended after providing educational services to Indian young people from 1890 to 1962. Comments on the School's closing: "School didn't last long enough." . . . "I want to come back to Santa Fe." . . . "They should have kept the School." These things were stated again and again and often by students who had some very serious problems. The actual departure of students again brought such expressions and copious tears from large numbers.

"Her References Are of the Best." (La Mar Lamb)

Shortly after the school's doors were closed, the State Department of Education, Office of the Superintendent of Public Instruction, wrote to the Institute, probably at Jerry's request:

This is to certify that Mrs. Geronima Montoya qualifies under North Central standards for both the elementary and secondary certificate with no shortages. Mrs. Montoya is a graduate of a regionally accredited institution and is authorized under regional accreditation to teach elementary subjects in grades 1 through 8 and may teach on a secondary level in the fields of art and English.

Mrs. Montoya's transcript of credits reflect a detail and proper training in the areas in which she is qualified to teach. Her scholastic achievement is above average, her references are of the best. (La Mar Lamb, Director, Division of Certification and Teacher Placement)

Perhaps because of this letter, Jerry was not summarily dismissed from teaching and was permitted to continue as a general elementary teacher of fifth, sixth, and seventh grades for a few months. Jerry describes the period as "a waste of time both for me and for my students."

"I Might Do More Good on This Assignment."

In December of that wasted year, exciting mail arrived for Jerry from the U.S. Department of State's Bureau of Educational and Cultural Affairs. The official envelope contained two letters: one from Frederick A. Colwell, chief of the American Specialists Branch, Office of Cultural Exchange, and one from Virginia E. Orem, program officer of the Division for Americans Abroad. Their letters invited Jerry to participate in a cultural exchange program in Europe for one to three months, beginning January 20, 1963, to display work, speak, and meet with groups in art schools. "The artist will be representing the American Indian, the American artist, and at times both," Virginia Orem's letter explained. While this was not tantamount to an appointment, it was an exceptional invitation. The program provided first-class international transportation, compensation up to a maximum of seven hundred dollars per month, and per diem reimbursement. The purpose of the exchange program, the invitation said, was to "make it possible for our posts abroad to have the services of outstanding Americans to assist them in developing good will, understanding and respect for the United States and its policies and institutions."

Jerry wrote back immediately to Virginia Orem:

I am interested and would like to participate as an American specialist in the State Department's Cultural Exchange Program.

May I have further information so that I may apply for a leave of absence from my present job and make plans regarding my family. If at all possible, I would like to take one or two of my boys along with me.

She also wrote a letter to Dunn:

Dear Dort:

Here is a copy of a letter I received from the State Department in Washington yesterday. This sounds exciting. What is your advice? I feel so unwanted here that I might do more good on this assignment. If I go I will need your help.

Dunn, as always, was quick to respond to Jerry's request for advice. She wrote back from her Los Altos home in California just after Christmas:

> I think the offer for you to go abroad as a representative of American artists is fine, and I hope you find your way clear to do this. It would give you real standing and make your trouble-makers sit up and take notice better than anything I can think of. . . .
>
> A few years back, the U.S. Information Agency or some other office of the State Dept. asked me to recommend an Indian woman artist who might be sent abroad somewhat as Kabotie had been. I sent in your name, and I think I mentioned this to you at the time. Then in the spring of 1961 I received a blank with your name with a request for my ideas as to your qualifications, including family. Enclosed is my copy of what I typed on the blank. I have just copied it off, as you may keep this as a remembrance of what I think of you. . . .
>
> . . . Of course such a trip for you would put a burden on Juan and the boys, but I just know how they'll all be glad to cooperate. In the end, it will mean much to you all, I believe, and maybe when the boys can be on their own for a while, you and Juan could go together on such trips. You both have a lot to offer both as people and as artist-craftsmen. (letter provided by Dunn)

Dunn included with this letter a copy of her reference. Frederick Colwell had written to Dunn on March 6, 1961, seeking to add Jerry to its list of possible American specialists "for use in the Department's Education and Cultural Exchange Program." They wanted a "brief and frank opinion of this person's professional and personal qualifications" and insisted that as "such specialists should represent America at its best, it is essential that both professional and personal qualifications be outstanding." To this letter Dunn replied:

> Mrs. Montoya . . . was a painting student of mine in the founding years of the Indian Painting Studio in which she now teaches. . . .

When I resigned in August 1937, she took over the Studio and has been there ever since doing creditable work through changing administrations. . . .

Mrs. Montoya is a distinguished lady in every respect—her career, manners and appearance. She is a person of natural attractiveness and unpretentious beauty by standards of either her own pueblo or discriminating society in general. She has remained a Pueblo Indian in the best tradition while acquiring through colleges, travel, and associations many of the best attributes of the well educated woman. She speaks perfect English and has spoken to groups of teachers and various memberships. In no circumstance does she give the slightest hint of the show-off or the "professional Indian"; and she has natural reserve that attracts response.

Moreover, Mrs. Montoya is the capable and sensible mother of elementary school-age sons and wife of a fine woodworker, also of the [P]ueblo Tribe. They own their own nice home and run it in orderly and apparently joyous fashion. Altogether they are an admirable family which would command interest and respect in any good community. (letter provided by Dunn)

Jerry's excitement and hopes were short-lived. On January 8, she heard again from Orem: "I regret to say," Orem wrote, "that the original request for an American Indian to visit abroad has been canceled" but that the Department expected interest in the project to be revived "somewhere in the near future."

"Don't Make the Journey Harder . . . by Your Grieving."

Just as the ceremonial calendar, ceremonial feasts, and religious celebrations marked changes of seasons for Jerry and Juan in their professions, so it marked changes in the family. By now, Juan and Jerry's eldest nieces, Antonita (Queen) and Elidia, and first nephew, Stuka, had all married, and Stuka and his Spanish wife, Margaret Roybal, had presented Pablo and Crucita with great-grandchildren, Carol and Frank.

On November 16, 1963, after Harvest Dance and before Thanksgiving, twenty-two-year-old Stuka was returning from

Albuquerque and the new home into which he and Margaret, Carol, and two-week-old Frank were moving. Aunt Shine's description of the tragedy is muted:

> Stuka either fell asleep or the car failed. Jerry remembers a funny sound when she was driving with Stuka one time when they went to Albuquerque. The car turned over three times and Stuka was dead on arrival at the hospital. I had to be the strong one. We brought Margaret to the hospital. She was in shock. It was very hard on my parents. Not only was he greatly loved, but he was the first grandson. I'm able to talk about it now. Our priest friends were helpful but it took me eight years to be able to talk about it.

The Rosary was said at Pablo and Crucita's house. St. John the Baptist Catholic Church in the pueblo, site of so many of the joyous marriages and baptisms, was the site of the requiem Mass. The entire family followed the hearse south to Santa Fe, where Stuka was buried with full military honors in the Santa Fe National Cemetery.

Grief washed over the family that year. Six days after Stuka's death, President Kennedy was assassinated. So distraught were they at both deaths that, for the first time in their lives, the sisters and their families did not celebrate Thanksgiving at San Juan.

Both the Catholic priests and the Pueblo religious leaders helped the family recover slowly from Stuka's death. "Indian religious leaders advise, 'Go to your house and be happy. Don't make the journey harder for the departed by your grieving.'" Still, Jerry did not paint or exhibit in the year following this tragedy. Grief, like love, was expressed in private in this family. It was difficult to find much to celebrate during this year.

"They Chased Me Out of the Institute."

The stalemate about reassignment continued. If Juan were to remain doing maintenance at the Institute, Jerry naturally needed to be nearby. As an alternative, the Civil Service suggested they move and teach together in Greasewood, on the

Navajo Reservation, but neither wanted to leave home, friends, and family. Finally, they reached resolution.

They chased me out of the Institute—well, they might as well have, because it amounted to that. They kept asking me, "Don't you want to retire?" And I asked, "At what?" And they said, "Oh, you'd be getting 250 dollars," and I said, "Gee, that's a lot of money!" Then I said, "No thank you. I don't want to go out to Tuba City or Greasewood." They had Juan going to one place and I was supposed to be going to another place! . . .

So finally they called me in and said, "Well, how about Adult Education?" And I said, "Where?" And they said "San Juan Pueblo," and I said, "Well, I wouldn't mind that!"

6
A GOOD AND
LONG LIFE
The Pueblo Ceremonial

The Sacred Obligations of Ceremonial Life

It might appear that the major focus of Jerry's life over this quarter of a century was her teaching in Santa Fe. This is untrue. However, to interweave the story of her ceremonial life with that of her teaching life is almost impossible (although that is what Jerry managed to do). There is a chronology to her teaching career, but her religious and ceremonial world responds not to chronology but to cycles. This timeless world is the core world for Jerry. Without her religious and ceremonial life, other activities would have little meaning for her.

Jerry danced in ceremonials for over seventy years without interruption; she was still dancing in her late seventies. She has spent more time baking bread, roasting chiles, holding babies in Pendleton blankets, and quietly attending ceremonials in rain, snow, and stinging heat than she has spent painting.

Jerry's family and ceremonial lives are inextricably interlaced. Family life seems to be experienced as an endless circle of births, deaths, marriages, gatherings, and prayers. Ceremonial life is also cyclical, each year another circle of songs, prayers, offerings, and dances that mark the turning of the world around the center of Pueblo life: the world navel, known physically and symbolically in the stone lying in the San Juan plaza.

In Pueblo tradition, important life-cycle events and religious ceremonials are celebrated with communal feasting. Each family brings food to share at the home of the celebrants. Women help serve the many guests. All are welcome on a ceremonial day; sometimes only family members and close friends gather for special family occasions, but often the entire village is invited.

"The Spirit and the Land."

In 1973, Jerry was invited to express some of her Pueblo religious beliefs at an adult education conference at the Oregon College of Education. Her descriptions provide a reverent and loving introduction to her ceremonial world, to the religious life of her people and their indivisible connection through ritual to the earth as mother of life:

> There is much spiritual life among the Pueblo Indians, especially where land is concerned. It is one of the greatest gifts that the Supreme Being gave. It is the source of all sustenance. From the earth the animals, plants, and water emerged. So, to the Indian people it is Mother Earth. The Earth is our Mother. She is the greatest provider, so we treat her with love, respect, and much reverence. By treating her in such a manner we gain health, happiness, and long life.
>
> The care and protection we give to the natural beauty and resources are different to the way non-Indians treat it. The non-Indians think nothing of burying irreplaceable beauty and natural wealth under steel and concrete. They have an indifferent attitude. An Indian will see beauty in a tree, an animal, or rock formation and will consider such objects as sacred and will try to preserve them. Man continually gives thanks to the Maker and to the plants and animals for allowing uses of them for survival.
>
> My people live in a landscape that stretches in all directions, even towards the sky. They have developed their way of life, their beliefs, and their ceremonies in accordance with the patterns and happenings on the earth and in the sky. They have created dances, songs, poetry, and ornamental designs expressive of the natural and

cultural phenomena. The rain, mist, lightning, and clouds are important themes in dance, song words, and ornaments. The clouds are equated with the Rain Gods who appear in rituals.

. . . The Harvest Dance is to give thanks to Mother Earth for the agricultural harvest of the year. We feed her the new crop and dance in her honor. We also throw gifts to the public. All societies take part, and each society has its own song.

The white man, meanwhile, can see only useless rock or shaggy old tree, which he will remove without hesitation. Indians sense the creative forces still alive behind each created object. They are aware of the fact that happiness, inspiration, and purpose in life depend on an inner awakening, call it spiritual if you like. Indians work with nature, not against it. The Indian tries to understand the natural forces and work within them. White man tries to control the natural forces and too often has destroyed the balance of the total design of nature, while trying to manipulate the environment.

People with true understanding of nature will often find a certain interplay of the elements essential for attaining religious communion.

For this religious communion, the Pueblo people have many sacred mountains, shrines, lakes, and ponds. They communicate with the Spirit by offering food of cornmeal and clothing and prayer feathers.

We have in our pueblo a center of the pueblo—called Nan Ochu Kwi Nan Sipú Pinge—Center of the Earth, as that is what it symbolizes. Ritual dances and other performances must continue to be initiated here, because this is the true center of the village. . . .

Center of Mother Earth is the source of all blessings and those are directed outward in all directions.

The three principal sacred points at which one may communicate with a spirit are the lakes and ponds, Center of the Earth, and the shrines.

One sacred mountain that stands out in particular is the Tsikumu P'in, which is located west of San Juan Pueblo. It stands out for the simple reason that pilgrimages by those in power are made more frequently and because it plays a larger role in the . . . religious life of my people as well as all other Pueblos.

Sun-Water-Wind of the North is visited far more frequently than

"Bringing out Sacred Water." Shiva casein by P'otsúnú, 1983.

the others. This is where one should go if he has a problem. In group ritual, also, the shrine seems to be the most prominent.

The Spanish-Americans living in the area of San Juan know about these pilgrimages, so much so that they often become quite anxious for pilgrimages to be made, especially during a drought season. They urge the people to make such a trip. That shows the faith they have in the Pueblo rituals. I'm sorry to say at this point that Tsikumu [P'in] is no longer for Indians only. Just recently—say in the last year or so—our people went on their annual pilgrimage and were shot at, so they really ran for cover in a hurry. Another time they asked ahead of time for clearance, so what did they find? White man waiting with cameras. Our people, of course, turned back disgustedly and disappointed and couldn't go to the top for their rituals. Now, I understand, the shrine is full of beer cans and other trash.

Desecration of such sacred places has inflicted deeper wounds on the Indian people than some of the worst political injustices. For the disappearance of such sanctuaries has left a vacuum which nothing the white man has to offer will fill.

We're thankful that we're on this Mother Earth. First thing in the morning when awakened is to be thankful to the Great Spirit for the Mother Earth; how we live, what it produces, what keeps everything alive.

There is a time when Mother Earth is asleep and nothing must disturb her sleep. No house cleaning, no chopping wood, no emptying of trash. This resting period is about mid-December, depending on the location of the sun. She is asleep until four days after the shortest day.

The East is the most important direction in daily life because of its identification with the sun, which is believed to be the fertilizing agent in nature. Thus the first act a Pueblo male performs when he gets up in the morning is to take a pinch of white cornmeal, throw it to the sun, and pray for long life.

Man had to continually give thanks to the maker and to the plants and animals for allowing use of them for survival. The essential water also comes from the zenith, Oepáa Makódé, and the nadir, Nansigenúgé. From above come snow, hail, or rain; from below come spring and well-water. Precipitation from the sky is associated with the cardinal directions, for snow comes from the north and the heavy rains come from the westerly Jemez range. The rain, mist, lightning and clouds are important themes in dance, song words, and ornaments. The clouds are equated with the Rain Gods who appear in rituals.

The veneration of all these natural features and forces has brought forth fine arts.

"I Like to Go to All the Indian Dances."

Jerry and Juan not only were busy getting further education, giving birth to and raising three sons, pursuing their teaching careers, and participating in their wider family life. They also had time-consuming obligations to each of their villages' ceremonial calendars. Juan held a lifetime position as one of the Sandia religious leaders, and Jerry danced regularly at both San Juan and Sandia. Obligations in the two villages were never-ending. When the Montoyas were not dancing, they were helping to prepare feasts or attending dances at other villages.

I think that as I got older, I appreciated the Indian religion more than when I was a teenager. At home, we just took our Indian way of life for granted. Mr. Faris, at the school, helped us to realize the beauty of our own culture. Even so, there are things I don't fully understand about Indian religion and probably never will. I'm just a lay person in my pueblo.

[*] I like to go to all the Indian dances in all the pueblos. Many of the dances are religious ceremonies and are very special and beautiful. I enjoy them so much that I could stay all day and watch. All religious ceremonials in our Pueblo and Hopi villages have special meaning for me. It gives me peace of mind and a spiritual lift.

I hate going to a dance where people are constantly jabbering. You go there for a purpose. To see, enjoy the dance and the singing. I wish that spectators would show more respect. I just like to be silent and enjoy the songs when I go.

Juan's pueblo, Sandia—a lot of people think that Sandia ceremonials and traditions no longer existed, but it isn't true. One anthropologist worked so hard to get something out of Juan [about the significance of religious activities in Sandia]. But Juan never gave the person any information. As an anthropologist, you would think that this person would understand a lot more than she does.

I like going to Zia for the Corn Dance. They don't have all those little ones, the children, dancing. The youngest are probably ten or twelve—not any younger. And the older clown at Zia always comes up to talk to us. And he says, "I've been doing this for seventy years and now I'm turning it over to the young ones." But he was out there just as strong as ever. He is gone now.

The Sunset Dance at Taos Pueblo and the foot races on San Gerónimo [Feast] Day—September 30—and the dawn Buffalo Dance at San Ildefonso are pretty special, too. It's really something at San Ildefonso when all those deer and buffalo and antelope are coming down from the east hills in the winter. It is a beautiful sight.

Cochiti has a wonderful winter Buffalo Dance. I could watch that Buffalo Dance all day and not get tired. They have expert choreographers. It is really classical. I think it beats any classic dance or ballet that the non-Indians have.

The Hopi dances in Arizona are pretty special, too, and have

(LEFT) *"Basket Dancer." Shiva casein by P'otsúnú, 1983.* (RIGHT) *"Young Buffalo Dancer." Shiva casein by P'otsúnú, 1983.*

always been important for us. We've been to all of the Hopi villages from Walpi to Moencopi. When I need a spiritual lift, that is where I want to be.

The San Juan Ceremonial Calendar

At San Juan, the ceremonial calendar starts around September 15. The winter group is in charge until February 15. Even for the Harvest Dance [*Tembée Shadeh*] in September, they still sing the summer cacique's song first. Whoever is leading that season has to be the first.

[*] I think we do [the Harvest Dance] to gain a good life for ourselves and for the people. It's a dance for everybody.

[*] When I participate in the Harvest Dance, I don't have to learn anything new because they are the same songs that have been sung for generations—how long ago, no one knows, but they are certainly beautiful songs—beautiful words as well as beautiful

melody. For Harvest Dance, we wear flowers in our hair and the men wear floral wreathes in addition to our usual ceremonial dress. The purpose of the dance is in thanksgiving for the crops—squash, corn, melon, chile, and all—and to feed Mother Earth at the shrine with the fruits of the harvest. Either the head clown requests the Harvest Dance or someone asks the head clown to sponsor it. We dance in four plazas. It's more ceremonial than it appears. But it's a throw [dancers throw gifts to spectators] and I have to buy things for it. I don't like it when it gets too commercialized and they have plastic things—plastic spoons and knives. In the older days it was all just harvest—squash and chile.

[*] We don't dance every year. [*] We did the Harvest Dance this past year. [*] One year we just got so soaked because it rained so hard. It just poured and we were dripping! We were dancing in water! There was lightning and thunder and here we were dancing in the water! Kinda scary! But it was so funny: once we finished there—where we feed Mother Earth—it stopped raining and when we went to the other plaza—the sun came out and we dried up.

[*] On Christmas Eve, there's the Matachine Dance in the afternoon and in the evening before midnight Mass. That's done again Christmas day.

When we, the authors, watched the Matachine Dance on a Christmas day, we stood in the south plaza in front of the pueblo house where Jerry was born. It was clear but bitterly cold with a wind sweeping down from the mountains. The sound of the fiddle and guitar players heralded the first view of the two lines of five men dancing. The dancers wore shirts and dark trousers, embroidered vests, and beaded moccasins; their capes snapped in the wind. Each wore a headdress with a high rounded crown shaped like a bishop's mitre, streaming with long ribbons. The leader, the *monanca*, wore a small cross at the top of his headdress. Each of the dancers carried a three-pronged stick in one hand and a gourd rattle covered with a colored handkerchief in the other. Behind the *monanca* followed a young girl, the *malinche* (Kurath with García 1970, 257), in a long white skirt, embroidered sweater, high wrapped white moccasins, and flowers in her hair. She was escorted

"Dancing Matachines." Shiva casein on dark brown colored paper by P'otsúnú, 1947. Indian Arts and Crafts Board, U.S. Department of the Interior.

by Matachine Tsáviyó clowns wearing white masks over their heads, jackets, and jeans and carrying long whips. They used the whips to "control" the boy dressed in a bull's skin who danced leaning on sticks as a deer dancer does. They danced several intricate figures rapidly and ended kneeling down in a pantomime of the bull's slaughter.

Kurath attributes the origin of the Matachine Dance to missionaries who hoped to replace Téwa dances with their own story of the Spanish conquest of the Moors. As was usual with Pueblo people, they managed to integrate the dance into their own ceremonial calendar and today it probably has pure Pueblo connotations in addition to Catholic ones.

"On the evening of Christmas day," explains Jerry, "there is the slow [Añgéin] Dance, then on December 26, the Turtle Dance. I don't think I could spend Christmas any place but San Juan. It's the only place I ever want to be for Christmas." The Turtle Dance, *Oekuu Shadeh,* is another men's dance that may be connected to the winter solstice (Kurath with García 1970, 131). It is named for the turtle shell rattles, *oekuu,* that are fastened to the legs of the dancers.

On the first of January, the officers of the pueblo are appointed, and on January 6, King's Day, they are installed and there is feasting. All the officers, from the governor on down, make a feast in their own homes and invite all the relatives. There's a Mass in the church. Friends usually arrive early to greet them with a shotgun salute or a song. There's dancing, too—any kind. Whoever feels like dancing can dance.

Then, in January, the war captain selects his dance—either Basket Dance or Cloud Dance. For Basket Dance the women are required to cut bangs as part of their hairdo. It's a very sacred dance. We wear embroidered black mantas and embroidered mantas or the black and the white Hopi mantas over the black mantas. We don't wear any silver jewelry because that was originally Mexican. At the end of the dance we say, "May you have long life." All of our dances are done for good and long life.

According to Kurath, the Basket Dance "promotes fertility in vegetation and in human beings by the symbolic power of baskets and of the women who carry them" (1970, 145). Bertha Dutton, the anthropologist, further theorizes:

> The baskets symbolize that which they contain: the food which preserves the life of the people. They contain the seed which is planted in the ground and which must be fructified in due time; the fruit or grain which the earth yields in response to the efforts of the people; the meal which is produced when the harvest of corn is ground; and, finally, the loaves of bread ready for the sustenance of the Pueblo group. The invocations for fertility which occur in the Basket Dance embrace not only the food plant life, but the human race, which must multiply and transmit the gift of life from generation to generation. A complete series of the scenes presented in this ceremonial would constitute the epitome of woman's life, her consecration to childbearing and the sustaining of the life of the pueblo. (1955, 15–16)

A typical Basket Dance, *T'un Shade*, took place in 1978. Early morning at the Cruz family house, Jerry and Aunt Shine were dressing

Crucita Cruz dancing Cloud Dance at San Juan Pueblo (1930s?). Family archives.

for the dance. They had both cut their hair in bangs across their foreheads. Around ten o'clock, two parallel lines of women and men dancers filed into the plaza. Both Jerry and Aunt Shine carried fine Hopi plaques or baskets in their left hands and fir boughs and rasps in their right. Jerry's youngest son, Eugene, was in the line of men. The ceremonial consisted of two dances in each of the plaza areas.

(LEFT) *Jerry with her partner in the Basket Dance, January 1978.* (RIGHT) *"San Juan Basket Dance." Shiva casein by Sôekhuwa P'in (Robert Montoya), 1988.*

In the first part, the women and men turned as they danced; the women moved their baskets and boughs alternately and slowly side to side while singing with the men. In the second part, the women knelt facing their partners and took out the rasps and scraping sticks that they carried with the fir boughs. They placed the sticks on top of the baskets and moved them side to side in rhythm to the men's singing.

As the dancing progressed, the winter sun etched the sacred mountains—Truchas Peak to the east and T'sikumu to the west. Around two in the afternoon, there was a break in the dancing for feasting at the individual houses.

Over fifty guests came to the Cruz house while Piedad and her daughters, Pauline and Elidia, Adelaide and her daughter, Queen, and Reycita served fresh bread, red and green chile stew, posole, and bread pudding, among other pueblo delicacies. Juan, as always, played games with all the children. After eating, the dancers went out again and continued through the rapidly chilling air until it grew dark.

After Basket Dance, the war captain turns over responsibility to the boys. If they want to do Deer Dance, they get permission from the hunt chief. It's usually in February. Bob and Paul and Gene have all danced Deer Dance. Then men turn it over to the ladies to select one, and they usually select Yellow Corn or Spring or Butterfly. Any of the ladies can dance because it's a social dance more than a ceremonial one.

Butterfly is a little more ceremonial, and it takes place in early spring or at Easter. One or more of the ladies go to the older head lady of the winter clan and say, "This is the dance we would like to do." Then she calls on the ladies and says, "This is the dance they want to do." Then we make a special visit to the war captain and say, "This is what we have selected." If we have Butterfly, the ladies select their own partners. It takes place in early spring or at Easter. Butterfly Dance is very expensive. You throw goodies—cloth etcetera—to the spectators and baskets of gifts to the partners.

We can dance at Easter, too, if we wish—one of those three dances. We're usually at San Juan for Easter.

Then the war captain is in charge again and there's nothing until June 13. That's the only time San Juan has a Corn Dance [*Khóhé'yeh*]— on St. Anthony's [Feast] Day. [*] We didn't go to the Corn Dance for a long time because that's the same day as Juan's village has their main feast, the Corn Dance, and so we dance there or prepare the feast instead. And all our friends would go down there, and when you've got your friends, you have to be there to feed them.

[*] June 24 is the regular feast day for San Juan, when they have Comanche and Buffalo dances.

The war captain and his staff are responsible for getting these dances organized. They used to have foot races, too, but no caciques are left to lead them anymore, and many of the songs are forgotten. Aunt Shine and I often dance Comanche. When Adelaide was sick, we did it as a prayer towards Adelaide's getting well.

June 24 is the feast day of St. John the Baptist, after whom San Juan Pueblo was named by the Conquistadores. Because San Juan Feast Day is celebrated close to the summer solstice, it may have esoteric connotations known only to the San Juan people. While they are usually up since before dawn preparing the feast, Jerry and Aunt Shine's day formally begins with a Mass in the Catholic

(ABOVE) *Jerry and Aunt Shine dancing the Comanche Dance in the south plaza, June 24, 1977.* (BOTTOM LEFT) *Jerry dancing with arrows in the Comanche Dance, June 24, 1977.* (BOTTOM RIGHT) *Jerry and other dancers dancing the Comanche Dance in front of the kiva, June 24, 1977.* (OPPOSITE) *Jerry and Aunt Shine (front, right) dancing the Comanche Dance, leaving the south plaza, June 24, 1977.*

church—as is true for them on all Catholic feast day celebrations in the pueblos. Frequently, the archbishop of New Mexico travels from Santa Fe, presides over Mass, and attends some of the dance. After Mass, the statues of St. John the Baptist, St. Anthony, and the Virgin Mary are carried by women into the north plaza and placed in a shelter of cottonwood branches. The first dance takes place in front of the shelter, and when it is finished, the dancers file into the shelter to light a candle or offer a prayer.

The Comanche Dance, or *Kwitada*, copies the Comanche dances and is thought by some to commemorate an early Pueblo victory over a Comanche raid two hundred years ago (Kurath with García 1970, 233). The men usually wear shawls as kilts, beaded leggings, knee bells, war bonnets or roaches of large, highly colored feathers, and paint on their chests, faces, or bodies.

The costumes have not varied since Jerry first began to dance. The women wear high-necked, long-sleeved, pin-tucked Téwa dresses in fine cottons—the dresses Jerry's mother so loved to make—with tall white deerskin moccasins, colorful mantas over their shoulders, red and green woven sashes binding the mantas to the now-full figures, and brightly colored silk-and-lace cloaks hanging down the back. Their hair is allowed to flow free; Jerry's has always fallen well below her waist. The dancing continues throughout the day. Aunt Shine recalls:

When we first got married, I use to dance every year for the Comanche Dance. And Gilbert used to be mad because Mr. Talachy's father [Mr. Atencio, an elder] used to always be coming the day before, the day before feast and ask me to dance Comanche Dance. I was always dancing every year that Comanche Dance.

Then, as Jerry explains, there is a lull during the summer:

After June 24, there's nothing again until September. In San Juan, we have the winter and summer moieties. I belong to the winter moiety. There are societies in each group, although a number of them have died out. There are both men and women in these societies. Now societies from which the caciques came are no longer functioning, and it makes things very difficult. To be a cacique, you have to be in a particular society, and they are the only ones eligible to continue.

"My Mother Told Us Never to Count Bread."

During the break between dances, Jerry would always return to the family house to feast and spend some time with the many guests who came to the house to be fed by family not in the dance. Usually, no one leaves without being given special loaves of bread or fruit pies.

I think we counted over two hundred people who ate at the house one year. We were so pleased that there was enough bread. My mother told us never to count bread. She said that this is true for bread especially. If you count it, you run out. But sometimes for feast days we do count it, and say "How many loaves did you put in there?" The older oven held more than our new one does, and we always want to make sure we have plenty.

Each year, Jerry and her sisters either dance or prepare the feast for San Juan Feast Day. She also participated in the Basket Dance, Butterfly Dance, Yellow Corn Dance, and the Harvest Dance. She and Juan attended the Corn Dance at Sandia and special dances and closed ceremonials at pueblos into which different members of the family had married. Sometimes they would attend other dances simply for their beauty and peace.

Participation in the ceremonial dance life of the Pueblo began fairly early for the Cruz sisters. Aunt Shine surprised her parents by dancing unexpectedly:

> I remember that one year I danced at a very young age, because that year I didn't tell my mother. We were still living in the [center of the] pueblo so I must have been about—I don't know—very young. I went to my aunt's house right across and they took me out to do the Buffalo Dance. My parents were so surprised when they went looking for me. They used to go dancing in the homes, you know, in the winter to entertain people. We went from house to house dancing [laughs]. That was the first time I think I danced. I must have been about six or seven.

While Jerry does not recall when she first started to dance, she does recall practicing for dances at school (of course, not under school supervision) and going home from the school to participate:

> I started to dance when I was in high school. Now they start younger. [*] I think I was in high school or had just left when I did the Corn Dance in San Juan. It was the only time I ever danced Corn Dance. Since then, I've danced the Corn Dance in Sandia.
>
> [*] Then we'd do the Basket Dance. Mother was dancing the Basket Dance so I just went along with her when she went to practice and just joined in. The Basket Dance is done in the winter.
>
> [*] I think Indian religion is hard to understand. The Catholic way is easier to understand. It's hard to be an Indian. It really is, because you have to do what they do in the pueblo and—it's just hard. You have to sacrifice a lot and you have to work hard. There's a lot of work involved in these ceremonies. So much of it is secret, too—and rightly so. It is for Indian people and no one else.
>
> Ceremonial dances really move you spiritually. [*] We want a good life for all of the people. That's the main thing for most of our dances.

Ceremonial dances do something for you. There's something about attending the dances. You just forget about all your worries and troubles and you just have—peace. It is a deep spiritual experience. We forget our worries. It's such a good feeling. Something about the dance makes our troubles go away.

7
AFTER THE RAIN
Adult Education and the
Crafts Cooperative

"We Taught Whatever They Wanted to Learn."

After her departure from the IAIA, Jerry's values of service to community, belief in traditional arts, love of teaching, and incapacity to do anything halfway all wove together in her new passion. Even though she had not envisioned her role as adult educator to the northern pueblos before it was offered her, Jerry claimed it as her own. She had learned more than art lessons from Dorothy Dunn, Chester Faris, and Kenneth Chapman; she had learned about teaching what students want to learn. Jerry brought this conviction to her new work. She quietly and implacably defied the government by teaching what her people asked for, not what was decreed. Later, realizing that an artists' cooperative would help all artisans in her village, she found land and money to realize that vision in the face of challenging economic and cultural realities. Again, Jerry saw herself simply responding to what was needed in the situation.

Jerry's new assignment began in autumn 1963. As adult education teacher for the Northern Pueblos Agency of the BIA, she was to work eight hours a day. Fortunately for Jerry, she had no fixed hours, no fixed curriculum, and in fact, no fixed pueblo. Jerry and Marcelino García, also "released" from the Indian School and now assigned as Jerry's aide, spent most of their time in San Juan because

(LEFT) *Jerry and Juan with their sons, on a trip to Catalina Island, California, 1964. Family archives.* (RIGHT) *The old San Juan Day School, which Jerry later converted into the first American Indian artists' cooperative in the nation.*

the governor of the pueblo had specifically requested an adult education program to raise the literacy level in the village. However, they were expected to work in the other seven northern pueblos, too.

"It was to my advantage, I think, because I learned a lot more from my people by talking. They were so nice and so good and so kind! And of course I was at home all the time." The lack of structure was a puzzle to Yíyá and the rest of her family: "'You have no hours!' Mother said. And Father would say, 'Why can't you stay here? Sleep here?' And Adelaide would always say, 'Well, when are you coming to eat?' Adelaide was a very good cook. She spent a lot of her time in the kitchen and always had meals for us."

San Juan classes were held in the old Day School building where Jerry had tried to fail fourth grade. Jerry and Marcelino began with five students. On a typical day, Jerry would prepare breakfast for the family in Santa Fe and then drive to San Juan to greet those students able to come that day. Jerry taught whatever her students wanted to learn: some wanted to improve arithmetic, spelling, and reading; others learned to weave from Marcelino, an expert; some began to teach other women pottery. When the younger working people arrived home from their jobs, they would gather in the old building for Jerry's typing class or for driver's education class, taught by a teacher Jerry had persuaded the BIA to send all the way from Albuquerque.

These evening classes gradually grew into a High School Completion and General Education Diploma (GED) program. Among Jerry's students were her youngest sister, Aunt Shine, now a dormitory counselor at the new Institute; Margaret, Aunt Shine's daughter-in-law and Stuka's widow; and Lorraine, Bill's wife. Aunt Shine and Lorraine completed their GEDs under Jerry's tutelage.

Jerry and Marcelino often covered more than four hundred miles in five days.

We were supposed to go to Taos, too. The Taos Pueblo Council didn't want adult ed but the people wanted it. The people kept asking, "Why don't you come to Taos and teach?" We had to tell them that the Council had to approve adult ed before we could go to Taos. We mainly taught at San Juan, but we went a few times to Nambé.

Along with visual adult education curriculum, Pueblo crafts were part of our adult education program because the people requested it and we saw the need for it. Through the various media of crafts we revived many of the older San Juan traditions. The arts and crafts developed out of the adult education classes.

We taught embroidery and weaving. Since I was adult educator for the northern pueblos with BIA, I had to go in to Santa Fe to the agency to attend meetings with all other department heads—realty, tribal operations, police.

We spent more time at Picuris. We hired some local people to teach them pottery and then we hired someone from Taos to teach them tanning [to make hides for drums and moccasins].

"People Came to Teach Us How to Read and Write Téwa."

In 1963 in San Juan the Summer Institute of Linguistics people came to teach us how to read and write Téwa. It wasn't part of the adult education program. But anyone who wanted to learn could come and learn. They taught us songs in Téwa. We don't have any more classes; we just go by what we have learned.

I should read the New Testament in Téwa more often because you can get out of practice. Mostly I read it in English. They keep telling us how complicated our language is and I never realized how complicated it is until we started learning how to read and write [it].

Jerry's older sister Piedad, who lives in the pueblo, helped in the translation of the New Testament into Téwa. And later, during the summers of 1969 and 1970, several members of the family worked with the Summer Institute of Linguistics in compiling a book, *Téwa Khawa: Téwa Names*, which contains some eight hundred Téwa names for women and men. Jerry did the illustrations, using line drawings of traditional Pueblo designs.

Always true to her love of learning and respect for the power of literacy, Jerry also took classes in teaching remedial reading and in teaching high school English.

"We Work alongside the People We Teach."

In an undated draft speech that Jerry wrote around this time—one of the many speeches she apparently made at different education conferences—she describes the operation of the adult education program in detail that reflects the dedication and breadth of the vision she brought to this venture:

Working with the alcohol problem are two boys that were . . . trained under OEO [Office of Economic Opportunity] for that particular area. One works in San Juan and the other in Nambé. Much is being done under this program but they need help. These two boys certainly are a big help.

Another source we have turned to is . . . the University of New Mexico. With their help we were able to hold several short courses in Business Management in San Juan. More intensive courses along this line are needed in all of the Eight Northern Pueblos.

From the Extension Service we are able to get all sorts of help as far as the learning situation goes. . . . These classes have been very informative and educational.

Most of the adults that come to AE [Adult Education] classes are interested in the crafts and that is what they want the most. They consider that as first priority. Secondly, they feel that they need English, arithmetic, spelling, vocabulary, reading and typing. They are not interested in receiving a certificate nor a diploma but mainly to have some knowledge of them for self-satisfaction and self-improvement. They want English mainly to be able to speak and converse with their non-Indian friends and customers. They want arithmetic so that they will know how to price their crafts and make change. All of the three R's have a part in every arts and crafts class without making it a formal class. It takes arithmetic to figure out designs, making a belt, weaving, embroidery, etc. etc. It takes spelling to label correctly. It takes English to read, write and converse intelligently. Of course, formal sessions are held for those that want it.

Non-Indians will think that it is mighty queer that some Indians are not interested in receiving certificates and diplomas. However, we must understand that the values of the Indians are very different to the values of the non-Indians. We must recognize and know these values in order to be of service to them.

Through arts and crafts classes in adult education in San Juan, the people organized an Arts and Crafts Co-operative which at this time is getting much publicity through the June issues of *Mademoisell[e]* magazine and *House Beautiful*. Requests for catalogs and price lists have been coming in. Likewise, orders for some of the crafts are picking up. . . . Economic problems for some of these people are being solved with the sales of their top quality crafts as well as from fashions, both traditional and modern.

There is nothing more gratifying and rewarding than to hear an elder say, "I didn't know anything until I attended adult education and learned how to do so many things. Now, I am able to earn a living with my weaving. Because I am old, I cannot get away from the pueblo, but I can work at home." . . . He can't keep ahead with orders for his traditional belts and sashes.

As part of our cultural program, Téwa classes are held in San Juan, Nambé, and Santa Clara. Learning to read and write the Téwa language is very helpful and beneficial to the Téwa speaking people.

We work very closely with the ABE [Adult Basic Education] professors from the Oregon College of Education in Monmouth,

Oregon. They have sent us many publications on adult education and on Indian people. The ABE professors visited our area in May and stayed for a week. Our adult pupils . . . gave them an Indian dinner, entertained them with Indian dances, demonstrated Indian bread baking and involved them in the actual mixing of dough and making and baking the bread. They participated in the Téwa class also. It was quite an experience and very educational for all concerned. They learned that the San Juan adult educators are not only book oriented but people oriented as well. They found that we work alongside the people we teach. Their problems are our problems. They were very impressed with the way we participate in community affairs and in the way we go about making home visits.

Family Changes

Jerry was grateful for the opportunity the job gave her to spend more time with her family in the pueblo. Pablo's health had worsened rapidly since his oldest grandson Stuka's death in 1963, the year before. His heart was overburdened physically and emotionally. Then Pablo broke his hip in June just after the San Juan Feast Day and couldn't walk well. He rarely left the house, where Crucita and Adelaide cared for him. The day he managed to walk outside into

(OPPOSITE) *Jerry writing on the blackboard while Marcelino García instructs Juan Trujillo in weaving a traditional sash during an adult education class in the old Day School. Family archives.* (ABOVE) *Jerry and Marcelino García (far right) with adult education students———, a needleworker, and Steven Trujillo, a basketmaker. Family archives.*

the chill air for the last time, the aspen had almost lost all their bright leaves and the clouds were gathered over Tsikumu. He died in October 1964.

And so once more, in less than twelve months, Jerry and her sisters followed the exhortation of their Pueblo leaders to "go home and be happy" so that they would not make Pablo's "return to the lake from San Juan" more difficult. This time, it was painting that offered Jerry a private and self-disciplined outlet for her grief.

The years immediately following Pablo's death brought more changes. Jerry's oldest son, Robert, married Eva Oyenque from San Juan; Jerry's first grandchild, Michael, was born; and Crucita, her mother, died.

Now, when Jerry walked over to the family house on her work days in the village, only her sister Adelaide was there to greet her. As the two sisters sat over lunch in the kitchen, they could still sense the presence of Pablo out on the back porch in the shade of the cottonwood trees and Crucita carefully bringing in pots from the fire.

"So the People Started."

By 1968, Jerry's adult education program at San Juan had grown from five beginning to more than sixty regular students. "Members came from all sections of the village and ranged in age from early twenties to late seventies with the common denominator being skill in making high quality craft objects."

I went the rounds with the Indian Commission on Adult Basic Education; they were trying to tell us that arts and crafts had no place in adult education.

[*] My job was supposed to be teaching the 3 R's. Down in Phoenix, that is the way the Washington bureaucrats put it at the adult education conferences. They said that the arts and crafts had no place in the adult education. We had quite an argument. They said, "You teach what the Indians need—what their need is." Well my people kept saying, "We are not interested in the 3R's. What we want to do is revive our pottery and embroidery and weaving" and certain things that they felt were dying out.

So that was the reason that Marcy [Marcelino] and I just went about teaching those things. I guess I am just stubborn. And of course I was always getting in trouble. I just went on; they kept insisting that we teach what the people need—and that is what the people kept telling me: "*This* is what we need!" So I went more by what the people wanted—better than following the directions from Washington!

Well, when they started learning and they started to excel in their work, we started having spring exhibits and we invited our friends. And since I know so many of the museum people and friends that came to the Studio and I happened to have their addresses, we started inviting them to the exhibit. So the people started selling their things from these little shows that we would have.

The program was becoming a center where the San Juan crafts-people could exchange techniques and ideas. Out of this experience grew the idea of organizing a cooperative, the first in any of the nineteen pueblos of New Mexico.

As Jerry said later in a talk at a U.S. Department of the Interior adult education workshop in June 1974:

> The cooperative venture at San Juan began in late April of 1968 when individuals at the adult education began selling their crafts and contributing a portion of their profits toward a cooperative in order to purchase materials more economically. By this time, the classroom had become a center for craftsmen. . . . We used the walls of the classroom as a product display area and began to set aside 10% of their craft income to purchase supplies at wholesale and to develop a central outlet. . . .
>
> On July 10, 1968, the group which had expanded to 23, formally organized themselves as a cooperative. The informal enterprise became a business. . . . The Oke Oweenge Coop, the name selected by the group, also adopted a trademark based on traditional Pueblo symbols. . . .
>
> . . . One of the unique aspects of the Coop is the fact that it was started with no outside money. It was self supporting and managed by the residents of the pueblo.
>
> The Coop began its operations in 1968 with $67. They earned $1,912 the first year and tripled it . . . in the second year. . . .
>
> From the start, we have worked to have all members—most of whom are middle-aged women with limited education—understand how and why the Coop operates as it does.

The Coop was an immediate success. Jerry knew that if the enterprise were to survive, they needed professional help and advice. She enlisted the aid of her young friend, Alfonso Ortiz, an anthropologist whom she had watched growing up and playing baseball with the San Juan Hawks. With Ortiz's help, the Coop obtained grants from federal and private sources to help begin operations.

I get a lot of joy out of doing, especially if it is for other people. I think that is why I wanted to start the Coop: to help do for others and help the ladies sell their crafts.

After they excelled in what they were doing, then I decided that we needed a better place to sell—not just working out of the little elementary classroom. We were so packed. We started to think about ways of getting a building.

Frank Cruz, the governor of San Juan, liked the idea—his wife, Helen, usually came to the classes too and he knew that we needed a building pretty badly. The only way we thought we could do it was to have EDA [the federal Economic Development Association] give us the money or build for us. So he and I went to see Joseph Montoya, the senator, in Santa Fe. We asked him if there was a way he would help us get funding for a building. . . . He understood our predicament and was most helpful in getting us the funding.

And we had to ask others—like Ed Smith [a geologist with the Eight Northern Pueblos] and Peter Chestnut [soon to be an attorney] . . . [who] were sent from New York. I guess it was the national organization—Association of Indian Affairs—that sent them out here. . . . They did a lot of footwork. They did all the writing. . . . Of course, they didn't know too much about our Indian people at that time, but I think they learned a lot! . . .

We would meet with them whenever they were available, and when we started to organize in '68 it became a regular coop. We elected our officers and then Peter wrote up the articles of incorporation and the by-laws and then we submitted that. So we got that going. We didn't have to wait too long. A state representative, Nick Salazar, and Leo Murphy [director of the North Central New Mexico Economic Development District] in Santa Fe, those people worked together to try to help us out with EDA and anything that we needed.

We got the grant for the building—I think it was 160,000 dollars.

"We Found the Place We Thought Was the Best."

When we had the good news [about the grant] and they said it would take a year or so to come through, then we started looking for a lot—how and where to build. We found the place we thought was the best. The person who owned that place had moved to Nambé so we went to the [San Juan Pueblo] Council. We asked some of the elders to see the owner to ask him if he would give us that piece of land. Some of our officers—like Mrs. Jackie Jones, myself, Mrs. Crucita Talachy and a couple of our elders, Mrs. Geronima Abeyta and Mrs. Luteria Atencio, went to Nambe to ask the owner—Mr. Talachy—if he would give us that land. The Council would give him another lot somewhere else.

Well he agreed. The way it was set up was that the Council would give us the tribal land but we had to run the Coop ourselves. They had nothing to do with it except that they would help us if we needed it. One of the councilmen remarked that we will fail within a year. Very encouraging! [*] How little the councilman knew that we have very dedicated members to operate the Coop.

The groundbreaking ceremony was held on January 16, 1973. Jerry gave the welcoming speech in which she reiterated that this was "something we have been looking forward to for a long time and now at long last that special day is here."

Andy Acoya, a Laguna Indian who is an architect, and Peter Chestnut worked together on the building. We told them what we wanted—that we wanted to be in keeping with the Pueblo style. So that was the reason that part of it is in a semi-circle. We said we would like for it to blend with the Pueblo architecture.

The new building bore no resemblance to the old Day School. A simple structure in a half-moon shape—reminiscent of a kiva and much like the ancient Pueblo dwellings unearthed in remote Chaco Canyon, probable ancestral home of the people—it was built close to the center of the village and dedicated in July 1973. The spacious and light-filled building had ample rooms for display, craft work, and meetings.

We just can't say enough of the people that started the Coop. They are such staunch supporters. They are the dedicated people. Those are the ones that are still on the board. They show up and work. We are not a million-dollar business but we are still above water anyway. Our summer is pretty good. Winter is slow. We had two types of membership but that has changed so we only have 20 percent membership now. [Members pay 20 percent of any sale to the coop.] The ones that join now, they join because they want benefits to attend workshops and buy fabric at wholesale price. They want to benefit from that but after they learn, then we don't see them anymore.

The Oregon Conference

While Jerry was in the midst of founding the Oke Oweenge Crafts Cooperative, she was invited to attend and participate in the convocation of a month-long adult education institute at the Oregon College of Education. The focus of the conference was "to acquaint current or prospective adult basic education teachers with the characteristic and motivational patterns of traditional American Indian culture and its relationship to the dominant Anglo society." Her participation was supported by the BIA Northern Pueblos Agency, whose superintendent wrote to the college, saying that Jerry had "been a very effective instructor as evidenced by her ability to motivate adults to participate and perform together and produce positive results consistently. . . . Mrs. Montoya is the sole adult education teacher with the responsibility of providing instruction to approximately 1,500 adults."

Ronald Chatham, director of planning at the college, wrote to her about her role in the convocation, entitled "Man and the Land." Her responsibility was to make an hour-long presentation, "The Spirit and the Land" (see chapter 6). Chatham hoped that she would focus on

the deep reverence the native American has for the land—how this feeling is expressed or shown by perhaps arts and crafts, poetry, the way people act and talk and feel, etc. You would perhaps want to use the Southwest culture for examples. Arts and crafts you might bring with you would be appropriate.

Her expenses were to be covered despite the minimal funds available for this convocation.

(ABOVE) *Oke Oweenge Crafts Cooperative, near the center of San Juan Pueblo. It was built in 1973.* (BELOW) *Jerry giving her welcoming address at the opening of the new building for the Oke Oweenge Crafts Cooperative, July 1973. Family archives.*

Adult Education ▪ 169

A few days before she was to leave, her second grandchild, Catherine, called "Póvi," was born to Eva and Robert. The family gathered for her baptism and then Jerry left for Oregon. Jerry's participation was so impressive that she was invited to become a working member of the adult education committee at a follow-up conference in Phoenix in February 1971. Jerry was delighted with the experience and the learning but not quite as satisfied with her contribution, as she wrote to her friend Helen Redbird, the program director:

> It was a wonderful four weeks and a time well spent. I gained much from the staff as well as from the participants.
>
> As far as my presentation went, I feel I didn't do as much as I could and should have. . . . I think we Indians take too much for granted. We think that everyone knows all there is to know about Indians. I found that this is not so. We Indians have to get on the ball and educate the public on the true facts of the Indians.

"We All Worked Together."

In March 1972, while the Coop was being finished and as Jerry was returning from teaching at Picuris, a severe allergy attack—Jerry was allergic to dust—made her decide to seek medical relief at the clinic at San Juan. By chance, the physician was there that day and responded not only to her need for relief from the allergy, but also to her request for a physical examination for pain that had been bothering her for some months. She was hospitalized the next day and, the day after, underwent a mastectomy about which she speaks little.

By the time Jerry recovered from surgery, the Coop was about to move into its new quarters. As she recovered, Jerry welcomed visitors to the open house for the elegant building, filled with San Juan craftspeople and their fine work. While this successful venture had its genesis in the termination of her twenty-seven years of teaching at the Indian School, she now believed that her talents were being best used in the development of this coop: "I believe that establishing the Oke Oweenge Crafts Cooperative was my most important and major contribution to my people."

San Juan was not the only pueblo to benefit from Jerry's creative organizational powers that year.

There were no other Indian coops at that time. So the Santa Ana Pueblo group came and wanted to know how we got started and we helped them along. And some of our Spanish people—just around our area—would come up to ask us to help set up the coops. I gave a workshop in Glorieta for Asian people from Philadelphia, Chicago, Los Angeles, San Diego—all over—who wanted to know how to start coops. Beautiful, beautiful embroidery that they did—so fine. [*] I don't know if any of them ever got started or not.

Also, while the Santa Fe Indian Market, sponsored by what was then the Southwestern Association on Indian Affairs (SWAIA), provided a much-needed two-day sales outlet for qualifying Indian craftspeople, most had few certain markets for their work, and no other cooperatives had yet been established. Concerned about this severe limitation, Jerry took responsibility for initiating an arts and crafts show, to be sponsored by the Eight Northern Pueblos.

After we got started, the eight northern governors wanted an artisans' guild for their people because only San Juan people could join our coop. And so at first we thought "Well gee, that is going to be competition," and Ed Smith said "That is good if you have competition." They founded the Arts and Crafts Guild next to the church and across from the coop. [*] It didn't last.

I was president there for seven years. We had committees and we had meetings and then we started to have shows. That was how the Eight Northern Pueblos arts and crafts fair [Annual Artist and Craftsman Show] got started. They planned to have a show in San Juan yearly and then, even after the guild finished, [people who had worked on committees] decided to have a summer show that moved from pueblo to pueblo. So many of them wanted a place to sell their work, a summer show. We all worked together as to what could be done. [*] Some of the pueblos are too small and it just got so big they couldn't handle the show.

Jerry and Aunt Shine, wearing their judges' ribbons at the Eight Northern Pueblos Annual Artist and Craftsman Show, mid-1980s.

The first show was so successful that it is now an annual event, every July, with Santa Clara Pueblo most recently taking a turn as host. Participants, however, need not be from the northern pueblos. Craftspeople from all nineteen pueblos and from the Navajo Nation take part. The show features generous prizes donated by friends and tradespeople. Social dances are presented by different pueblos.

Busy as she was organizing the opening of the new Coop and initiating the Eight Northern Pueblos Annual Artist and Craftsman Show, she still accepted a second invitation to address the convocation of the Oregon College of Education. She also, around that time, agreed to speak to an adult education workshop run by the Albuquerque Area Office of the Bureau of Indian Affairs. Representatives of twenty-four tribes were present, among them fellow speaker Lloyd Kiva New, her longtime philosophical opponent. Jerry's address concluded by spotlighting the development of the Oke Oweenge Crafts Cooperative.

With business as it is now, we are beginning to make work schedules to make sure that the store is handled properly with enough clerks to handle sales and visitors. We are receiving many foreign visitors, as well as other Pueblo people and Chicanos that are interested in starting coops, so we are serving others as well as our own.

By the end of 1973, Jerry had worked for the Bureau of Indian Affairs for thirty-eight years. Juan retired that year and began doing occasional construction and carpentry work. Occasionally, he would even work on a project with his son Robert, then a partner in Mimbres Associates, the Santa Fe architectural firm that he co-founded. Now, at fifty-eight, Jerry decided to retire. Perhaps her illness contributed to this decision, in her late fifties, to leave government employment. She had completed another cycle of her life, her second career, after a decade of service. "I thought of waiting until I was sixty, but then I decided, 'Why wait?'"

8
PRETTY RARE OBJECTS
Painting

Living a Creative Paradox: Tradition and Individuality

The word "traditional" means different things in different fields. Archaeologists, anthropologists, and art historians all disagree among themselves. Individual tribal members differ as well. Is "tradition" a workable concept? Is there Indian art or are there only Indian artists? We have a strong but not exclusive appreciation of the kind of painting that Jerry, her sons, and her students have evolved, and we only offer a context in which to appreciate Jerry's experience and approach to traditional Indian art. She is living out unanswerable questions rather than providing answers.

For Jerry, there is such a thing as "true tribal tradition" in painting. There always has been. Her experience of making and teaching traditional Indian art has more to do with her tribal and cultural experience than with style or media. Dorothy Dunn also sees art as part of life for Southwest Indians:

> Especially in the Southwest, painting is so much a part of all the arts
> through which the Indian identifies . . . with the universe that to
> consider it apart from the whole is like examining a single thread
> drawn from a tightly twisted cord. One art intertwines with and sup-
> plements the others; they all unite to join the Indian and his earth

(ABOVE)*Pictographs found behind San Juan Pueblo from which Jerry has frequently taken inspiration for her paintings.* (OPPOSITE) *"Kossa." Shiva casein on dark brown colored paper by P'otsúnú, 1947. Indian Arts and Crafts Board, U.S. Department of the Interior.*

and sky and his unseen gods. Art is a way of life. It has a bearing upon every aspect and detail of the Indian's existence—birth, nourishment, rest, growth, learning, work, play, reproduction, healing, even death. (1968, 29)

Jerry, as a self-described traditional artist, has painted when she could and felt like painting. Painting has been woven in with her other worlds. Some artistic honors she has received almost in spite of herself, but her first priorities have been to tribe, family, and students. Her second priority has been her own art.

Always there, never explosive, essential to her heart's operation, her art has held a steady beat. Her apparent lack of ambition has puzzled some non-Indians who have wanted her to achieve maximal recognition, but Jerry has found no frustration in her approach. She just loves to paint, usually at the kitchen table and often late at night. And she has been happy to earn supplementary income.

Certainly, she has participated with her family in every Santa

Fe Indian Market for decades, letting housework slide while she works furiously in the early summer to prepare a portfolio to sell in August in her booth under the portal. Most of her exhibitions and sales, however, have resulted from invitations. Her entries into juried shows have stemmed more from her sense of obligation as an art teacher and practicing Indian artist than from individual need for recognition.

Choice of Subject Matter and Style

Jerry distinguishes between traditional and nontraditional art. "Traditional" for her connotes harmony in color choice, balance, repetition. She values subjects that derive from Pueblo life: natural phenomena, ceremonial and religious rituals, daily activities. She believes subjects should be treated with dignity, respect, understatement, or gentle humor; their choice should never violate the secrecy of religious life. Her paintings also all imply timeless repetition and cycles; they feature no specific individuals; they use tribal symbols and Mimbres designs with fidelity. Jerry is not a sentimental painter. Nor is she prone to nostalgia: "I paint because I like to do it. Painting gives a good feeling. I like to sit down and see what I create."

Jerry's painting is for her a pleasure and another form of service to Pueblo ideals. Paintings should, she believes, support, communicate, and teach the best communal, religious, and spiritual values of the community that gives the painter life. She sees each artist, including herself, as one small part of a community, to which allegiance should come first at all times. According to John Anson Warner, Pueblo pottery designs reflect a similar desire for collective aesthetic allegiance:

> Pueblo culture witnessed a high degree of conformity and social control, which was tangibly expressed in the uniformity of pottery styles. At no time would an individual potter wish to stand out from her peers as different, for that would violate the ethic of uniformity which was cultivated so strongly. (Warner, in Wade 1986, 173)

In contrast, what Jerry seems to find most difficult to accept in Indian paintings are high chroma expressions with arresting gesture (a distracting indication, perhaps, of self-seeking individualism?) and expressions divergent from the solidarity and perceived social expectations of conservative tribal life, beliefs, and social mores.

> I like the traditional art because it's really Indian. I can't see why many of the painters want to paint like white men. I like to paint so people enjoy the painting I do. Many of the paintings being done now, I couldn't live with.
>
> [*] Bob uses modern techniques, but he doesn't lose that purity of Indian. I don't know how else to say it. He keeps the feeling. I think because Bob and Paul have participated in hunts and ceremonials and the secret dances, that when they do those paintings, it's done from within. Paul is more a quiet type and his paintings are very peaceful, whereas Bob is a very lively person and his paintings show that liveliness—like his mudheads [divine Zuni interpreters and guardians of kachinas].

It is a continuing source of puzzlement and sadness to her in her later years that many younger Pueblo people, particularly artists, seem to be pursuing their often oppositional individual visions above

Jerry with her abstract painting "Sun," 1950s. Family archives.

the collective; what does not dignify or reflect the best ideals of the community detracts from the good of the whole, making everyone in this collectively based society suffer a little. Edwin L. Wade has commented that, among conservative Pueblo people, success as an artist is suspect because it removes the individual from the realm of the collective and possibly the collective good. Better to be a good farmer (1986, 246–248).

Jerry has never said that modern or postmodern work is bad, inappropriate, or otherwise negative; she has simply said that she doesn't like it. As with her own history, she believes that what is negative is better unspoken—or painted or sculpted. To perpetuate it so would not benefit the community.

> If what artists see and feel fits comfortably within the common cultural context, then they are very likely to use conventional materials and styles to manifest their art. But if artists see the world in terms of a vision or emotion that is remote from their societies, then they are inclined to invent new styles and to search for new materials that make it possible for them to realize their uncommon and individual visions as works of art. (Highwater, in Wade 1986, 225-226)

Jerry is clear—and succinct—about her choice of subject matter and how it has changed over the years. She says that when and what she wants to paint is a matter of feeling. "The way that we feel: we want to put that into our paintings. I would tell my students, 'Enjoy it and paint how you feel about certain things.'"

Her subject matter explores themes she has pursued all her days: home life at San Juan, animals including *avanyu* (serpent) and turkey, pictographs at San Juan, pottery designs and lines of all Pueblo styles, and ceremonial life.

> I get inspiration from Mimbres designs and the dances and home scenes especially. I started out painting home scenes, like baking bread. Then, in the fifties, I did more pottery design and then just birds and then, by the sixties, I was using Mimbres figures and petroglyphs. You just feel like you want to do something.
>
> I like to paint what I see: the beauty in the birds and in the animals and the plants and then in the dances. There is something beautiful about our Indian way. I just feel that maybe people will enjoy seeing these things too. People can see and learn what it is like in our lives.
>
> [*] We paint nature a lot. We use our cloud symbols and our rain symbols: things like that, because they are part of nature. And I think the Indian people always go back to nature because they appreciate Mother Earth and they appreciate the wild life: the trees and the animals and that sort of thing.

Perspective and shading seem unnecessary for the symbolic, spiritual content.

> We try to portray [nature] in symbols. You know, you see us paint trees that don't look realistic. Then we do the cloud patterns, the rain, and the birds. And then we paint the deer in a very stylized way rather than trying to make it realistic. I don't try to be realistic like a camera.

Colors tend to be harmonious, drawn from Pueblo ceremony, and often earthen. Jerry uses casein tempera, an opaque water medium, almost exclusively and rarely blends one color into another. Textures are usually consistent within a painting: a painting done in brayer (with a sponge roller) is all brayer; a painting with incisive lines has color worked into the areas defined by the lines.

I always use casein tempera. It's a water-base paint and not the transparent watercolor. Bob uses the same thing. I have one pet brush— one I like especially. I use an eight or ten. I paint the solid areas before I paint the fine lines. Sometimes I use a different brush for different colors. I also use sponge to create a different type of painting. The only other thing I use is the brayer method, and when I use that, I use printing ink, which has an oil base. I enjoy doing the brayer—seeing what I can get out of that big roller, trying to get fine lines. I paint at San Juan when I need space for brayer paintings.

Of course, there are times when you think "This is no good." You put it in the trash can and start another one. [*] Sometimes it comes out the way I want and sometimes it doesn't. Sometimes I paint over and over again. And then sometimes it still doesn't look right and I paint over again until I'm satisfied.

When I paint, I have in mind what I want to do. I sketch first and do many sketches before I start painting. And then I have pages and pages of sketches. Then I will go back and paint the ones I like. I have to be in the mood to paint. A painting mood.

One Family, Many Expressions

In the post–World War II era of modernist individualism, a condition of pluralism exists in American Indian arts. No one particular sort of individualism predominates exclusively. Instead, there are at least three different types prevalent in the modern Indian art world; modernist individualism that is a continuation of and elaboration upon reservation art traditions; modernist individualism that employs new forms of expression but retains Indian symbolism; and modernist individualism that is assimilated into the mainstream Euro-American art.

Some Indian artists prefer to retain the community-oriented art traditions that were so pronounced in the reservation period.

Traditionalist Indian painting, for instance, which still persists today, has large numbers of both practitioners and consumers. At the same time, many Indian individualists are emerging who retain reservation-art traditions, but are expanding and elaborating upon them. (Warner, in Wade 1986, 197)

Jerry's attitude toward Robert's and Paul's paintings and Eugene's carving shows what she values in the evolution of painting in her community. She is appreciative and approving of their work and especially takes delight in the feeling for Pueblo life that each son creates. Ironically, while Jerry taught so many Indian artists from 1937 through the early sixties, her own sons, having gone to St. Michael's High School, did not receive formal instruction. As with so many of the Pueblo artists and craftspeople, their work has evolved from being raised with a painter and a woodworker for parents.

Her two painter sons could be said to represent both ends of the Studio-style spectrum—or two forms of "modernist individualism": Paul uses the traditions of the Studio exclusively; Robert expands on those traditions and extends into new forms and styles. Jerry

(OPPOSITE) *"Taos Pueblo." Shiva casein by P'otsúnú. (Date unknown) Purchased by the de Young Museum in San Francisco in the 1950s. Family archives.* (ABOVE) *"Forest." Shiva casein by P'otsúnú, 1950s. Family archives.*

loves both: the bolder, experimental forms of Robert's work and the fine details in Paul's miniature paintings of ceremonials. Jerry speaks of her sons having a deep familiarity with the Pueblo way, particularly the ceremonial, because of their regular participation in the religious cycle. She believes that this imbues their painting with feeling and understanding.

Robert integrates his architect's skills with his ongoing experience of ceremonial participation at his father's pueblo of Sandia. While he began in the sixties by painting realistically, he tired of painting "chamisa bushes, arroyos, and piñon-studded hills" and decided to try Indian subject matter. He has painted only Indian subjects ever since, evoking the feeling of tribal experiences, both mythological and ceremonial, and exploring stylized animal motifs. He rarely paints home scenes as Jerry does; his early childhood was not spent in the pueblo, although as an adult he has actually lived in one (Sandia) much longer than Jerry.

Robert's color spectrum resembles and differs from his mother's: he seems equally comfortable with representational and symbolic color combinations, hardly ever using primaries. He works predominantly with ceremonial colors: subtle earth tones, blues, blacks. He rarely uses pure blues, rendering sky and water in ritual turquoise. Occasionally, he experiments with shades within a single color for a face or pot. He works almost exclusively on white board whereas his mother works with colored papers.

In contrast to his mother, who reveals her quiet and occasional humor as readily in her paintings as in her speech, especially in her portrayal of certain animals like the skunk and turkey, Robert shows his humor only in his speech. His paintings are serious and rooted in the numinous world of emergence myths (explaining the journey of the people into the present upper world), fertility figures, hunting rituals, and nature, particularly night skies.

Robert plays with style as comfortably as Jerry works within Studio styles. With equal facility, Robert uses perspective and almost sculptural realism, abstracted and established design motifs and landscape, and both daring and conventional composition. He often combines blended color areas (applied with dry brush) with highly defined areas (applied with fine brushes) and abstraction of two- or three-dimensional figures with highly sophisticated design elements. He rarely works solely with an abstract design, often working pottery motifs into his figures of dancers and hunters or figures from myth. He likes to overlay his abstracted or simplified structural forms, such as kivas, with larger contrasting forms that break up the more representational areas into mystical parts of larger designs. Robert seems to express, through varied content and form, his lack of interest in and transcendence of the unforgiving divisions among "traditionals," "moderns," and "postmoderns" in the American Indian art world and its critics. Robert describes his own experience as a painter as highly personal:

> In order to exercise my creativity and imagination, I paint. To record or document Pueblo ceremonialism, legends, traditions, and stories, I paint. To relieve stress, express happiness, and because I feel good about myself or my environment, I paint. I do not paint if I am troubled or unhappy about something.
>
> Most of my painting occurs during late afternoon and night time hours—often continuing into the early morning hours. . . .
>
> My process is very private as I allow very few people to visit when I paint and I encourage no visits. . . . Although it is important for people to see the transition and development of a painting, I am not comfortable with allowing the viewing of any work that is in progress, allowing this only in special instances and for special people. . . .
>
> . . . I treasure my privacy to the stage of almost being selfish with my time, and it is during this privacy that I am most creative.
>
> I like my paintings to show harmony in design, scale, and color. The subject matter usually illustrates the harmony of Pueblo ceremonialism and traditions. The preparation and practice of ceremonialism and tradition is to maintain harmony in life and environment. There are so many ways to describe a ceremony, tell a story or a legend, and I pursue these by using my imagination, creativity, and detail.

Quite different from Robert's work, Paul's miniature paintings portray the harmony, timelessness, and beauty of ceremonial life with realistic yet formalized dance figures, often set within a symbolic context without shadow or specificity of setting. His figures float free of all except minimal perspective and planarity. Figures stand inside arcing rainbows or dance with measured motion in front of kivas, surrounded by unpainted space. Faces are not individualized but are part of a repeated design. Paul seems concerned with describing the collective experience and the subsuming of that experience to higher, invisible energies. Robert describes his paintings with enormous admiration:

> Paul has expressed his feeling for dance since he was a small boy; today he continues to do so through his paintings. . . . He believes dance to be an integral part in the circle of ceremonial harmony. He has documented and illustrated the art of dance in realistic and stylistic form. . . .
>
> Between 1978 and 1982, he lived on the Hopi Reservation in Arizona. Many of his dance scenes reflect a Hopi influence, and his treasured opportunity to observe Hopi ceremonialism at its most beautiful.
>
> Paul also deeply values the influences of his mother's art, Pueblo dance and ceremonialism, and the styles of artists like Gilbert Atencio, Joe H. Herrera, Fred Kabotie, and José Toledo. They were traditionalists in their respective cultures and so, too, is Paul as he uses his art as a true documentation of the harmony in Indian ceremonialism.

The Place of Beauty and Harmony

Any attempt to discuss the function of art within the Pueblo culture presumes that "function" is a relevant concept within that culture. Traditional Pueblo artifacts were often functional, some materially, others spiritually. In a world view in which balance and harmony with nature are paramount, function can also be expression of beauty, harmony, or balance.

What seems important for Jerry and her sons when they look at their own and others' paintings is whether they see beauty as they define it within the tribal aesthetic. They are committed to portraying what they perceive as harmony, balance, and beauty in content, form, and color. Not one of them has ever intentionally created a painting that overtly expresses inner or outer conflicts in content or style. The harmony, beauty, and balance each puts into a painting is not a wistful portrayal of an unlived ideal or a reflection of

(ABOVE) *"Emergence at the Sipapu." Shiva casein by Sôekhuwa P'in (Robert Montoya), 1988.* (BELOW) *"Corn Dance." Shiva casein miniature by Póvi Ta' (Paul Montoya), 1983.*

lives without grief. Each has known difficulty and loss. However, what they choose to express in their art is a re-creation of what abides and heals their lives, what uplifts creator and receiver.

While they repeat images and forms, and take pleasure in working with themes that please others, their work suggests the archetypal, not the stereotypical. Jerry can explore the same bird form many times; in so doing she is motivated not by Studio mores or market preferences but by enjoyment. Each painting has autonomy and integrity.

Expression of tribal life through art forms, "functional" or otherwise, is a given among many Pueblo people, certainly in the Cruz and Montoya families.

> There are no artists, as commonly known, in Indian society. Anyone may be a painter, a craftsman, a singer, a dancer, or a creative participator in some capacity. To be an artist is taken for granted. . . . To paint a symbol in a bowl . . . to sing or create a song, or to dance is as ordinary and natural an occurrence for an Indian as to plant a hill of corn. (Dunn 1968, 29–30)

Skills are learned formally or informally. Once again, the creative paradox is held between adherence to collective expectations and individual variation within a form.

There is no differentiation of art from craft at Santa Fe Indian Market where the family shares a booth in the center of the portal. Aunt Shine's embroidery hangs beside Jerry's, Robert's, and Paul's paintings; Aunt Shine's granddaughter's beadwork is on the table; Eugene's delicate carved and painted wooden hummingbirds, just like his father's, stand in a pot on the table; Piedad's leggings are laid out across the street in the San Juan coop booth. Aunt Shine's embroidery, named "best of division" many times, has been purchased by museums that consider it the finest contemporary example of traditional Pueblo embroidery; Aunt Shine is equally comfortable, however, using traditional symbols for contemporary dresses for purchase by Indians and non-Indians.

Listings

Jerry's reputation had grown so much by 1946 that she was invited by the School of American Research to be included in a list of Indian artists for the school's joint publication with the University of New Mexico Press, *An Art Directory of New Mexico.* The correspondent asked Jerry "to provide adequate information on yourself as a New Mexico artist." Because she was both an established artist and a

"Corn Gods." Shiva casein by P'otsúnú, 1983.

well-known teacher of so many of the successful Indian artists by this time, she was asked for "minor" additional help. "We are also enclosing," the request continued, "a list of Indian artists for you to assist us in completing. Will you check their addresses, star the most important ones and cross off any who are not working in the art line and add any others you may think of."

The same year, the director of the University of Oklahoma Museum of Art, Oscar Brousse Jacobson, also wrote to Jerry with a similarly all-encompassing request:

Dear Jerominia [sic]:

I believe I told you that I managed to secure one of your paintings from Mr[s]. Hall Adams while I was in Santa Fe. They seem to be pretty rare objects and you did not show me a single one of yours while at the school. Now I would like to have your biography to go with it . . . : what tribe, where born, education, art education, where you have exhibited, and other things of interest up to today. . . . I have assembled the largest collection of Indian art in America for our Museum of Art [this was inaccurate]. . . . To go with each of the paintings that we have, I am preparing a biography of the artist and if possible also a photograph of them. So I also want a photograph of you. Do you think I am asking too much?

(Above) *Jerry at Indian Market with one of her abstract design paintings, 1976.* (Opposite) *"Petroglyph Hunter Kachina." Shiva casein by P'otsúnú, 1978.*

Jacobson did not mention to "Jerominia" that his plan was to publish her work. In 1950, C. Szwedzicki, the leading art publisher in France, announced a "forthcoming portfolio" called *Les Peintres Indiens d'Amerique* (*American Indian Painters*) with introduction and notes by Oscar Brousse Jacobson and Jeanne D'Ucel. Sale of the limited edition of 750 copies was to take place by private subscription, for forty-two dollars a volume. The price of both volumes, now treasured by collectors, was seventy-six dollars. None of the artists whose works were included was paid.

Jacobson's biographical note that accompanied Jerry's painting of a Matachine dance was remarkable for its condescension and inaccuracy:

> The little lady has had an interesting career and has been a fine influence in the renaissance of Indian art in the Southwest. . . .
>
> Teaching is an exacting and exhausting profession. It leaves little time for creative work. Most of Geronima's time has been devoted to her talented pupils. Her production is therefore rather

small and her works are rare. We had to search a long time to
secure a suitable example for our University art collection, and
Geronima, being an Indian, gave us no help whatsoever, in
locating or showing any of her work. (vol. 2, listing 48, page
unnumbered)

Jacobson did not offer Jerry a courtesy copy of this premium publication. In fact, like most of the artists included, she did not know of
its existence until thirty years later. Precisely this sort of experience
made many Indian artists wary of outside interest in their work.

Exhibits, Prizes, and Purchases

The earliest painting Jerry can remember selling was a casein watercolor. She sold it for three dollars to Helen Blumenschein, an artist
and daughter of the Taos painter Ernest Blumenschein. Another
early painting, an earth-toned mural-style work, was purchased by
Dorothy Dunn. Soon, Jerry's work began to be exhibited: first, of
course, in the Studio's annual May exhibit at the Museum of Fine
Arts of the Museum of New Mexico, in Santa Fe, then at the Golden
Gate Exposition. During Jerry's twenty-five years of full-time teaching, she painted whenever she could find time. The prizes and purchases soon began to come. She received her first in New Mexico

at the 1954 Gallup Intertribal Ceremonial, where her mother had also received a blue ribbon.

Her reputation as an artist began to spread. Jerry exhibited that year at the Brooklyn Museum, in Detroit, and in Chicago, as well as in the West. In December 1954, the de Young Museum in San Francisco exhibited Jerry's *San Juan Pueblo*, purchased by a prominent San Francisco family as a gift to the museum. In 1955, she was awarded the Purchase Prize by the Indian Defense Association of Central and Northern California, San Francisco, for her tempera painting *Cutting Wheat*. This painting, too, was donated to the de Young. For the award and its honor, Jerry received $22.50.

"I Can't Seem to See My Way Clear."

Although Jerry was exhibiting—whenever she could—in shows at the Museum of New Mexico, she was unable to accept her first offer of a one-person show at the Paul Schuster Gallery of Art in Cambridge, Massachusetts. In March 1957, Schuster invited her to give a show of paintings, prints, and cards in March or April of the following year. He wanted, he said, to include many paintings. There would be no charge for the exhibit, but she would have to pay for the announcements and the postage. She was unable to accept the offer, however, regretfully replying to Schuster:

> At present, I can't seem to see my way clear to prepare an exhibit for May. My classes are such that I am kept busy all day long and of course my evenings are taken up with my family. On Saturdays I go to school in Albuquerque.
>
> Last Christmas I took leave with the hopes of painting but I was sick all during my leave so I got only one painting out. I have a few small paintings. If you wish to see them, I'll send them to you.
>
> With every spare time I have, I am going to paint . . . and maybe could arrange to have an exhibit at another time. I am awfully sorry that at this time I am unable to send you enough paintings for an exhibit.

Jerry's work was even absent from the 1958 May exhibit at the

Museum of New Mexico; she had not had time in the preceding months to do any painting. But eighteen of the forty students who placed in the exhibit were Jerry's; of those, five won prizes.

"She Has Incorporated Symbolism . . . with the Modernistic Style." (Santa Fe Scene)

By 1959, Jerry was able, at last, to mount a one-woman show in the Hall of Ethnology in Santa Fe. The show opened on August 10 and ran for about a month. Given the tumultuous developments that were afoot in the Indian art world, what the brief review of her show says about her traditional and modern trends is noteworthy:

> Viewing P'otsúnú's paintings one can see that she has incorporated symbolism of the Indian design with the modernistic style of painting. She has experimented with different color background papers, allowing them to determine color blendings of her designs. The subjects are most interesting and revealing. (*Santa Fe Scene*, August 15, 1959, 2?)

Most of the pieces sold for modest prices: the *Avayu* for thirty dollars; the *Butterfly* for forty. The prices seem to have been determined as much by the size of painting as by any other criterion.

Challenged and Recognized

The most stressful years of her teaching career, 1961 and 1962, were among the most successful for her as an artist. At the same time as her conservative philosophy of Indian art was being strongly opposed at the University of Arizona summer classes Jerry attended and at the school itself, and even as her job as head of the Studio was being phased out, she was fêted for her paintings.

In 1961, Jerry again placed in the Museum's annual Indian arts exhibit with *Long Hair Kachina*, which was awarded a purchase prize. Further, despite her waning position at SFIS, Jerry was the only Indian artist included in the 1962 edition of *Who's Who in American Art*. Similarly, Jerry was the only woman award winner in a large

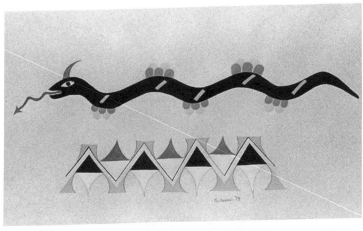

(ABOVE) "Avayu." Shiva casein by P'otsúnú, 1979. (BELOW) "Mountain Sheep." Shiva casein by P'otsúnú, 1980. Dry brush method.

field of artists accepted for entry in the 1962 Seventeenth Annual American Artists Exhibit at the Philbrook Art Center in Tulsa. She received a second award of seventy-five dollars for *Hunter's Dream*, and first prize for student entries went to her Zuni student Roger Tsabetsaye. First-prize winner was a young Navajo, R. C. Gorman.

The Philbrook competition held more than one reward for Jerry. In May, she received a letter (addressed to "Mr. Geronima Montoya") from the U.S. Department of the Interior informing her that her two paintings *Harvest Dance, San Juan Pueblo* and *K'ohsaa in the Pueblo*, also in the exhibit, had been purchased by the Bureau of Indian Affairs.

In that same troubled final year of the Studio, Jerry also made time to exhibit at the First Scottsdale Annual Painting Exhibition at the Scottsdale Arts and Crafts Center in Arizona. Jerry, who was apparently being fired for her determination to continue teaching traditional art, had her entries classified as "non-traditional." The exhibit accepted five of her paintings: *Spring* (casein, fifty dollars), *Lifeline* (casein, forty dollars), *Gossip of the Day* (casein, forty dollars), *Flying Duck* (watercolor, fifty dollars), and *War Captain* (watercolor, sixty dollars). All sold.

In March of the same year, the two paintings *K'ohsaa in the Pueblo* and *Harvest Dance, San Juan Pueblo* were hung in the exhibit hall of the State Department in a show of contemporary American Indian art in May. In the Second Scottsdale Annual Painting Exhibition, in 1963, three of her works were accepted: *Basket Dance, Long Hair Kachina,* and *Drought.* The first two were purchased by the Museum of Fine Arts in New Mexico. The work of some of her students was also exhibited, including that of Robert Tsabetsaye and Gilbert Atencio, Atencio a prizewinner with his painting *K'ohsaas Making Medicine.* In the winter of 1963, Jerry's work joined that of nineteen other artists, including Josef Bakos of Santa Fe, in an invitational exhibit at the Symbol Gallery of Arts in the Old Town section of Albuquerque.

In that year following Jerry's dismissal, and while IAIA was voicing its wish to have Indian painters open themselves to the world art community rather than confine themselves to regionalism and Studio style, the State Department invited Jerry to display twenty paintings in Amerika Haus in Nuremburg, Germany. Amerika Haus, a cultural center supported by the U.S. Foreign Service, then sent the paintings on a six-month tour of Munich and other European cities. This exhibit was followed by one in the German American Institute in Regensburg and by an exhibit of two paintings, *After the Rain* and *At Dawn,* in the Indian show at the Museum of Fine Arts in Santa Fe.

One artistic success and irony followed another. Jeanne Snodgrass invited Jerry in that same year to submit information for a one-page entry in the biographical dictionary *American Indian Painters*, ultimately published in 1968 by the Museum of the American Indian, Heye Foundation. In 1965, Snodgrass, by then curator of Indian Art at the Philbrook Art Center and apparently open to both schools of painting, mounted a special show honoring Geronima C. Montoya and her former students who had received national acclaim. In her letter of invitation Snodgrass wrote:

> Because I have respected your talent and the many years you have devoted to the education of so many artists, I would like to make a proposal to you. I would like to invite you to have a show at Philbrook. My further idea is this. The show would be mainly your own but in addition I would like to show one painting by some of your former students. If you should accept my invitation, I would appreciate your help in selecting the former student artists to invite.
>
> I believe this would make a very fine show. It would be an attempt to honor you and because so many of your students think so highly of you I believe they would deem it a pleasure to assist.

Eighteen of Jerry's paintings were included, in a range of media, from casein to brayer, as well as Jerry's favorite tempera. There were also paintings by Narciso Abeyta, Gilbert Atencio, Harrison Begay, Joe H. Herrera, Oscar Howe, Charlie Lee, Eva Mirabel, Ben Quintana, Percy Sandy, Theodore Suina, Quincy Tahoma, Roger Tsabetsaye, and Beatien Yazz. Jerry does not comment on this, but the show may well have provided dignified public acknowledgment—at a painful time when her ties to the Studio were being severed and her values attacked—of her contribution as teacher and artist to the development of American Indian art.

Jerry's other paintings from this period, exhibited in rapid succession, showed versatility. Some were traditional in subject and style; others highly stylized; still others, symbolic abstractions. In March 1965, she held a solo show at Yonemoto's Fine Arts Gallery in Albuquerque of the same paintings that had toured Europe the year before. Yonemoto himself noticed the new developments in her work that year and declared the show one of the most exciting the gallery had ever had. According to the unidentified reviewer:

"Kossa." Brayer abstract by P'otsúnú, 1982.

Many leading Indian artists have been her students and attribute
their success to her talent and inspiration.

. . . This show was well received by thousands of Europeans. . . .

Her paintings are not only in the traditional Indian style. She has developed a new style in her symbolic paintings done in various media. Many of her subjects have a touch of humor and show the artist's great imagination as she portrays the animals and moods of the Southwest Indian. (*Albuquerque Tribune*, March 4, 1965)

In September 1965, Jerry exhibited three works, *Acoma Bird, Rain Maker,* and *Funmakers,* at the Bismarck Art Association in North Dakota as part of the National Indian Art Show. And in 1966 the Museum of the American Indian produced a series of lithograph greeting cards of her paintings (for which Jerry received a flat fee of fifty dollars).

Four years after her quarter-of-a-century association with the Studio and at the height of the new movement, her own work was being acclaimed for its new direction: she was lauded for her "departure from tradition," for her free style and modern techniques. For example, a favorable review of her exhibit at the Valley National Bank of Española reported that

this was one of the best attended and most popular exhibits. . . .
. . . The latest paintings by Mrs. Montoya show a departure from her early so called "traditional" style. She now concentrates on individual symbolic motifs, many of them from ancient pictographs recently found at the ruins at El Guique near San Juan. They are done in a free style using a variety of modern techniques. (Suzanne K. Boss, *Southwest Association on Indian Affairs Quarterly,* Winter 1966, vol. 3, no. 4, 15–16)

The following year, in January 1967, Scripps College, affiliated with Claremont College where Jerry had studied, asked her to provide some of her and her students' recent paintings for an exhibit. She had no student work available but sent twelve of her own pieces, almost all of which sold. Carl H. Hertel, director of the Scripps College Art Gallery, was delighted, calling her work a "unique and beautiful addition to our exhibition" (personal letter, Jan. 20, 1967). Once again, the paintings showed a variety of content and styles: some were ceremonially inspired, such as *Harvest Dance, Blue Corn Maiden, Rain maker,* and *K'ohsaa at Play;* others, such as *Game of*

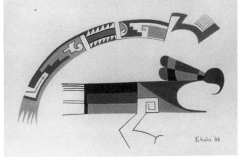

(LEFT) *"Fox." Shiva casein by P'otsúnú, 1982.* (RIGHT) *"Bird and Rainbow." Shiva casein by P'otsúnú, 1982.*

Plenty and *Mountain Sheep Hunt*, were inspired by daily life; traditional symbolic designs were developed in *Arrow Heads* and *Clouds and Lightning*; and her favorite animal and bird motifs appeared in *Shy Rabbit, Butterfly, Bird in Flight,* and *Frightened.*

In July 1967, she had another local one-person show at the Mesa Public Library. A great pleasure for Jerry in this show was not simply the exhibit and sale of her own work but the inclusion of three pieces of pottery by Crucita—a bowl, candlesticks, and a plate—and embroidery by Aunt Shine—including a manta, a belt, and contemporary clothing.

> The dominant feature of the exhibit is the use of subjects, symbols and emblems of the Pueblos. The paintings, however, display an enjoyable versatility. Some are traditional in subject and execution; some are highly stylized—colorful symbols beautifully drawn; others are abstractions; a few are in a primitive style that is appropriate for her pictographs.
>
> There is variety in media and techniques too. (*Los Alamos New Mexican,* July 27, 1967)

In 1976, year of the U.S. bicentennial, Alfonso Ortiz, who himself was making a presentation, made it possible for ten members of the San Juan artists' cooperative to be invited to Washington,

D.C., to the Tenth Annual Festival of American Folklife. Co-sponsored by the Smithsonian Institution and the National Park Service, the festival drew together traditional skills, music, and lore that made up the mosaic of American life. Each week highlighted a different Native American culture. The group of Pueblo people demonstrated their arts and crafts and celebrations. They performed Basket, Turtle, Cloud, and spring social dances. Jerry's sister Piedad demonstrated belt weaving; others demonstrated bread making, pottery, silver smithing, woodcarving, beadwork, and basket making; Jerry demonstrated traditional painting techniques and styles.

Two Family Shows

In 1975, the Oke Oweenge Crafts Cooperative held the first of what they hoped would be a series of "Indian family art shows." Jerry, Robert, and Paul joined with seven other family members to mount a family exhibit of crafts and paintings at the Coop. Piedad, her two daughters Pauline and Elidia, and Reycita exhibited weaving, traditional clothing, embroidery, and crochet. Aunt Shine exhibited twelve pieces of stoneware and traditional pottery—displayed next to Crucita's pots—and embroidery of traditional red, green, and black Pueblo patterns on handwoven materials, as well as traditional Pueblo clothing. Her son Bill and his wife, Lorraine, exhibited a variety of crafts, including two carved deer dance figures, a carved kachina and corn maiden, and silver jewelry. Paul, Robert, and Jerry covered the walls of the Coop with their markedly different paintings. Adelaide remarked, in Téwa, to her daughter, Queen, that her art form was cooking—preferably on Crucita's wood stove.

In the autumn of 1982, another family show was held in Palo Alto, California. Jerry, Robert, and Paul exhibited over thirty paintings, most of which sold. They also had exhibits together in 1986 and 1988.

The Recent Years

In her seventies, Jerry continues to paint and to explore the themes that have fed her imagination throughout her life. She still exhibits every year at the Santa Fe Indian Market and watches her sons continue to develop as painters.

> I lose track of time when I paint. I like to just sit by myself and paint. Though I didn't mind Juan being there. He'd just sit quietly. Sometimes I turn on the recorder and play Indian music.
> I listen to tapes of Indian songs when I am painting. The beautiful Téwa words seem to give me ideas for my pictures. Harvest Dance especially has wonderful words of nature—the stars, the clouds—all are what I would like to capture, but they don't quite come out the way I picture them.
> Juan would suggest names. He would sit there and watch and he would say "Call this painting 'such-and-such.'" He was good about that.

Juan is no longer there to listen to the tapes of Indian music as she paints or to name her paintings as he always did. But her paintings still flow from the same steady place within her.

What was laid down sixty-five years ago when Jerry and the other Indian students first encountered Dorothy Dunn, Kenneth Chapman, paper and watercolors, tempera and charcoal has abided. The creativity nourished in those years of exposure to new media has fed them all their lives. We shall never know to what extent the blossoming of the creativity was the direct result of Dorothy Dunn's vision and later Jerry's. We shall never know how much of the students' fidelity to painting was engendered by the same kind of inclusive and collective spirit that allowed many Pueblo people, like Jerry, to integrate Catholicism into spiritual lives already replete and rich.

Perhaps Jerry—a student about to become artist and teacher, with a vision of service and of guiding her students to their artistic heritage—simply developed her talents amidst necessary circumstances, among a group of homesick, resilient children with a cultural sensitivity to the creative process, within a receptive and fertile environment in Santa Fe, and at the time of a federal policy attempting to redress past wrongs of enforced alienation. What we do know is that those years and Jerry's tribal experience and beliefs have inspired

(ABOVE) *Some of the hundreds of booths at Indian Market, 1982. St. Francis Cathedral and the Sangre de Cristo Mountains are in the background.* (OPPOSITE ABOVE) *"Turtles." P'otsúnú, 1983.* (OPPOSITE BELOW) *"Butterfly Design." Shiva casein by P'otsúnú, 1983.*

her art for over half a century and provided her and others with an infinite source of inspiration and possibilities. "I guess my paintings are kind of bold, like me. Like *Under the Portal* [see color section]— it's just a person there without much detail. But bold!"

We also know that the institutional battlegrounds drawn up to keep traditionalists like Jerry and the modernists and postmodernists apart seem to be gradually losing their aesthetic and historical relevance. As Gerhard Hoffman, an American Studies specialist at the University of Würzburg, comments:

"Lizards." Shiva casein by P'otsúnú, 1983.

That the conflict between proponents of the traditional and champions of the modern/postmodern has abated lately appears to be less a sign of growing insight than of increasing helplessness in the face of ever more rapidly changing modes and styles of painting, the exhaustion of the cult of the new, and the extensive reconsiderations and reevaluations of art and culture. (in Wade 1986, 266)

It may now be time for the dualism and opposition between artistic camps to give way to a more fluid appreciation of the paradoxes and extraordinary contributions of American Indian art and artists.

9
TOO MUCH TO DO
Later Years

In Retirement

Jerry moved with more fluidity among her worlds now that she was not accountable to an employer. It never occurred to Jerry to stop working. Instead, her professional life continued to quietly transform. So too did her family life. About joyous events and family crises, Jerry speaks rarely and briefly, having already responded to each event with integrity and determination, regardless of outcome. She has never been a passive bystander in the presence of forces with which she disagrees. She brings to most situations what she brought to her dismissal from the Indian School: a profound and active belief in immutable principles and higher forces at work. Although her firm convictions have not always been received well by those around her, those tribal and Catholic beliefs have provided a foundation that grounded all fears, grief, and chaos and have given her inner strength to continue the service that structured and brought meaning to her days. From family to tribe, from student to teacher, from painter to juror, service has remained the thread that has woven together the sometimes worn yet always seamless fabric of her life and worlds.

"From One Generation to Another."
(Senior Citizen Commendation)

Like so many years in Jerry's life, 1976 brought sadness along with honors. Adelaide, like Crucita in her quiet authority, was now the matriarch. However, she had not felt well for some time. Despite her daughter's professional nursing advice, she delayed going to the Public Health Service Indian Hospital. When she finally did, the diagnosis was cancer. She had immediate surgery. Although the prognosis was not hopeful, she proceeded with debilitating chemotherapy. That summer, Jerry and Aunt Shine danced for Adelaide on San Juan Feast Day.

August brought the Smithsonian trip to Washington for Jerry (see chapter 8). Much as she loved to travel, she was unhappy about leaving New Mexico and her sister. While she was there, Jerry painted a scene of the willows, with the San Juan men and women fetching water at the spring—the spring to which Adelaide had carried Jerry in her shawl when both were children.

Adelaide's health steadily declined. By 1978, she did not venture out of the family house often. Jerry was greatly distressed. "After Christmas she really went down and was helpless. She wouldn't go

(OPPOSITE) Jerry, after hanging a selection of her paintings early in the morning, Indian Market, Santa Fe, 1976. She is dressed in traditional San Juan costume. (ABOVE) Reycita and Adelaide at the Eight Northern Pueblos Annual Artist and Craftsman Show, 1976. (BELOW) Jerry and two of her sisters at the Santa Fe Indian Market, 1976. From left to right: Aunt Shine, Jerry, and Piedad in front of Jerry's paintings.

(Above) *Jerry painting in her "studio," the family kitchen, with Juan watching, late 1970s.* (Opposite) *Jerry with Povi, 1988.*

and live with anyone. She preferred being at home. I worried so that I couldn't get anything done for myself."

Piedad had retired from her job at the Indian Hospital, where Queen was still employed, and returned to San Juan, where she lived with Pauline across a small arroyo from Adelaide. They spent much time with her. She died in the hospital in April, the same month her mother had died ten years before. Now the family house was empty except for feast days.

The family had hardly begun to recover from Adelaide's death when illness followed for Pie, Pauline, and then Juan. All recovered but it was a trying and demanding time for the family.

In the midst of these uncertain days only a few months after Adelaide's death, the entire Eight Northern Pueblos Council saw fit to recognize Jerry's unending contribution to her community. On May 30, 1979, the Council gave Jerry and other outstanding community members a special Senior Citizen Commendation:

We praise and honor you today for the knowledge and wisdom you

have given to our people. The leadership and the compassion you
have passed on from one generation to another is something to be
proud of.

What we are today, is what we were taught by you, our mothers
and fathers. . . .

We are truly grateful and thankful to the Great Spirit for giving
us such wonderful people such as yourselves and we thank all of you
for everything.

As close and inspirational as her family was for Jerry, these comments must have seemed as much like words she would have
addressed to her parents and to Adelaide as words that she was
hearing about herself. However, it was undeniable that her values had passed on to a new generation. All three sons were now
working in service professions that, like those of their parents,
benefited their people. Paul was a criminal investigator for the
BIA police. Shortly after Adelaide's death, he was able to arrange
a transfer from the Hopi Reservation in Arizona back to New
Mexico. At first, he lived in the house next to the family home
in San Juan; today, he resides in Laguna Pueblo. Eugene, currently
a juvenile probation officer working out of Española, again
shares the Santa Fe house with Jerry. Robert, together with Eva

(ABOVE LEFT) *Jerry and Juan with Póvi, their granddaughter, at her First Communion, 1982.* (ABOVE RIGHT) *Paul Montoya, 1976.* (OPPOSITE) *Jerry standing with Robert in front of their paintings in the family booth under the portal, Indian Market, Santa Fe, 1976.*

and their two children, Michael and Póvi, moved in the early eighties from Santa Fe to Juan's house in Sandia Pueblo to be closer to his new job in Albuquerque. Robert and Eva were later to be divorced; for Jerry, as a traditional Indian and Catholic, this event was painful.

The Loss of Juan

In the winter of 1982, Juan—husband, teacher, fisherman, father, grandfather, and religious leader—went out in the family pickup to cut Christmas trees for the family. Aunt Shine and Jerry talk about the night before he went out for the trees and what happened the next day:

> Jerry: He was always so happy to help with the children. He loved children. We would go to a grocery store—and maybe the mothers would have their kids in the cart—and he would go up to the kids and talk to them. I said, "One of these days, the mother is going to slap you [laughs]!"
>
> Aunt Shine: That night before he died, we were here. We had Erin, remember? Carol had just had Frankie. Erin was wearing some

old patchy pants. Every time she went by, Juan would pull [at] the pants and laugh at her. And that's what I remember the last night we were here: teasing.

Jerry: He usually got three [Christmas trees]. One for them [Aunt Shine's family] and one for us.

Aunt Shine: Three. One for San Juan.

Jerry: And I was telling that day that he was leaving—it turned out to be a real nice day and all that week—it snowed, and snowed and snowed. So I was telling him, "Why don't you ask Gilbert to go with you?" "No, I don't want to bother him. He is probably working because today is a nice day." So he went by himself. He didn't want to bother anybody.

After Juan cut the Christmas trees, he climbed back into the truck and quietly passed away. Aunt Shine remembers: "We were here that Monday night. That is what I remember about him. Remember, he was sitting on this chair? Every time Erin went by he pulled at the little pockets and he would laugh at her."

Jerry and her family's grief was deep and private. Jerry found the house very quiet—too quiet—yet she continued to paint and to show her work that year. "I had a show at the Governor's Gallery, at Legend's Cafe, and then a show in Phoenix—and then the Mesa

A family fishing trip, late 1970s. Left to right: Juan, Jerry, and their sons Eugene and Robert.

Public Library in Los Alamos [and then the benefit for the] Colorado Springs Opera Festival, in '83."

In 1985, three years after Juan's death, the Santa Fe Indian School (now once again a boarding school for Indian students) held a dedication service for new buildings to be named after Juan and another Indian leader, Delfin Lovato. The invitation to the dedication invoked the memory of Juan as a "spiritual leader and family man. . . . May his example guide our youth."

"I Just Figure If They Want Me, I'll Serve."

Jerry has been active on many boards and committees, particularly those of the Southwestern Association on Indian Affairs.

> I was on the board of SWAIA from '74 to 1992, until I resigned last summer. I was on the educational committee . . . the membership committee . . . standards committee—and was chairperson for the

clothing contest. Then they decided that they wanted a non-Indian to be chairperson of the Indian clothing contest.

Jerry was disturbed by several changes in policy that the SWAIA was taking. The first change was in the last word of the name, from "Affairs" to "Arts." This was not merely a symbolic change; it signaled the Association's increasing focus on the development of Indian art rather than on issues of more general concern to Indians. Along with that shift went a decision to make the Santa Fe Indian Market a larger affair. Despite being an artist, Jerry's primary concern was always the welfare of the entire community, and she did not sit easily with any activity that did not take the whole into account.

I didn't like the direction that they were taking. They changed their name in the first place. It's all on Indian art and I didn't like that. I would rather see [SWAIA] turn and help in the case of, like, taking care of the [Indian] Hospital. Or, instead of paying these big-time singers from South Dakota and where ever they come from to have a pow-wow, I would rather have them use that money to lobby Washington, to try to improve the health service for the Indians. SWAIA was started to help Indian people where they needed help. But it is not working that way now. It's all for art. I believe in the art too but there are places for that too.

While Jerry might have had differences with SWAIA's philosophy, the Association honored her with a plaque "in appreciation for your dedicated service as a SWAIA Board Member."
Her community service has extended well beyond SWAIA:

I don't know why I accept so many volunteer jobs. They ask me and I just figure if they want me, I'll serve. Sometimes, when I would go to answer the phone, Juan would say after me, "No more committees!"
I was on the New Mexico Commission on the Status of Women, when it was first organized. And then the All Indian Pueblo Council Tricentennial Committee from '79 to '80. And then of course president for the Northern Arts and Crafts Commission from the time it

Jerry relaxing after the family painting show in Palo Alto. Seventeen Mile Drive, Monterey, California, 1982.

was organized. I served there for seven years. And then on the National Endowment [for the Arts'] Arts and Crafts Task Force. I was on that in 1980 and '81. And then the San Juan Tricentennial Committee. I was on the board of trustees at the Wheelwright [Museum, in Santa Fe]. I was a docent there at one time too until Adelaide got sick and then I had to leave that position. I have been a judge many times for the Eight Northern [Pueblos] Show and in Phoenix for one of the exhibits they had and then SWAIA.

I'm advisor to the Indian art museum [Museum of Indian Arts and Culture in Santa Fe]—on the advisory panel and the education committee. We advise on what type of things to show and decide whether some of the pieces they want to show are sensitive to the Indian people. Sometimes people will show things that Indian people don't like. And sometimes things need to be returned to the Indian people, not shown in the museum.

Then recently I have been appointed to be on the board for the [San Juan] Agricultural Coop—a farmer's coop just for San Juan. The man that started that said that the Council members decided that they would like to see some woman on the board since the women seem to succeed in doing things like that. What they want to start out with is raising alfalfa. Now they are planting corn, chile, tomatoes, gourds. They also raise cattle and turkeys.

Recently, I was asked to help out with another board: the Poeh Center in Pojoaque [Pueblo]. I told them that I just couldn't be on that but they kept writing to me that I am on the committee. So I went to a couple of their meetings but didn't go any more. I've also recently been appointed to be on the tourism committee [of the Eight Northern Pueblos Council].

Jerry's responsibilities to the Oke Oweenge Crafts Cooperative continue to take her there one day a week, and often more, for meetings and classes. The Coop members elected her a lifetime member and lifetime chairperson of the board of directors.

She continues to receive honors. Beginning in 1987, the Santa Fe Community Foundation, which gives awards in the names of outstanding Santa Fe citizens, established an annual Geronima Cruz Montoya Arts and Humanities Award. In establishing the award, the foundation stated that Jerry "has made significant contributions to the quality of community life" and cited her teaching at Santa Fe Indian School and her leadership of both the Oke Oweenge Crafts Cooperative and the Eight Northern Pueblos Artisans Guild as "outstanding."

In 1992, the Museum of Indian Arts and Culture in Santa Fe honored her with a whole day's celebration of her artistic and teaching contributions to American Indian art.

The most recent honor was from the National Museum of the American Indian (NMAI), of the Smithsonian Institution, in 1994: an "Art and Cultural Achievement Award, recognizing an individual's lifelong commitment and contribution to the development, maintenance, and perpetuation of Native culture and community" (nomination form, NMAI Award Selection Committee). Jerry was given an all-expenses-paid trip to New York City in October 1994 to receive her award at a reception in conjunction with the opening of the NMAI George Gustav Heye Center.

(LEFT) *Piedad Antoine, holding her prizewinning crocheted leggings at Indian Market, 1977.* (RIGHT) *Family picnic in the Valle Grande, 1980. Jerry is the background, cooking beans.*

"I Composed Some Music."

Jerry's energies are not solely devoted to civic service. Her early experiences with Antonio García's choir led her back to participate in the San Juan choir and allowed her love of music to extend for the first time—in her seventies—into musical composition.

> I belong to the San Juan Tewa Women's choir. We didn't belong to it when they first started and then when Shine and I were invited to join, we said, "We don't live in San Juan and won't be able to come and practice or attend Mass there." And then they said, "Well, come when you can." But since we made a commitment to be part of the choir, we said it was not fair to the choir members to not go regularly, so we've been going to practice and then go to the services.
>
> I composed the "Lord Have Mercy" and "Gloria" section in Téwa. I did another tune to other Masses that we sing. I did another tune for the "Gloria" for one that we call the Western Mass. There is no "Gloria" to that one so I did one for that and Sister [Ann Szabo] still has to put it together. I hope she still has the tape. She moved from San Juan.
>
> I made it up by just going around and trying to make a tune. I

sang it and recorded it. Then I gave it to Sister and she listens to it and puts it in notes. We surely miss her. She is the one responsible for getting us to compose the Mass in our Téwa language.

Playing music is the one thing that Jerry says she wishes she had pursued in her life that she has not:

I wish I'd kept up with the music. That's one thing I wished I had kept learning and playing. Mainly for my own pleasure. Not to perform for anybody, but just for myself. I got interested when Virginia Clark was my roommate at SFIS. She was a music teacher at the Indian School. That's how I got so involved with Santa Fe Concert Association too, selling concert tickets. I got interested in the music and enjoy it.

"Tekakwitha Might Become the First American Indian Saint."

A serious new religious interest for Jerry and her sisters, all of whom are as devout and active as Jerry, is the work to canonize a young Indian woman revered as a saint by many Indians. Jerry speaks about Tekakwitha with reverence:

Blessed Kateri Tekakwitha might become the first American Indian saint. She was born in Auriesville, New York, in 1656. She was persecuted for her faith and fled to St. Francis Xavier Mission near Montreal in Canada. She died on April 17 [1680] when she was 24. Because we want her to become a saint, we make an annual pilgrimage—the National Tekakwitha Conference.

Tekakwitha wasn't very well at all. She had pock marks on her face from scarlet fever. But when she died, her skin just cleared up. It was a miracle, they say. She had no marks at all.

[*] She has been declared "blessed." And I guess that is the next step before they become a saint.

[*] The Tekakwitha Conference is like a spiritual conference. I was nominated to be on the Board but I guess they had more people from the reservation—so I didn't get on, which is ok. I was glad in a way because it would be another board!

The first conference was in Albuquerque and Juan and I attended that. It was in '81 and since then I've been going to all the conferences. We usually stay in dorms on college campuses [in different states]. When we had the conference in Syracuse, New York, we went to her birth place, to where she was baptized and where she died. It was a beautiful, beautiful trip that we took to see where she lived—the St. Regis Reservation.

According to its own brochure, the Tekakwitha Conference is designed to "unify Native American Catholics while respecting tribal differences; to empower Native American Catholics to live in harmony with their Catholic and native spirituality; to promote and maintain on-going communication and involvement between tribes, the . . . conference and the Catholic Church" and to involve Catholics in the various activities around the canonization of Tekakwitha.

To attend the conference every year, Jerry usually travels by bus or plane with her sisters and other Pueblo members. In 1987, Pope John Paul II visited the group in Arizona. This was a moving and momentous occasion for the sisters. The advent of the annual conference is an important event in their calendars and has made August even busier than previously, when it was usually given over to the preparation of paintings for Indian Market.

"Just a Down-to-Earth Person."

In her late seventies, as Jerry continues to paint and to exhibit her work, she also sustains close connections with her large extended family, volunteers at the San Juan coop as its lifetime chair of the board, acts as an advisory member for the Museum of Indian Arts and Culture, makes a home in Santa Fe for Eugene, attends Mass regularly, participates in the ceremonial life of San Juan, and attends ceremonials at nearby pueblos. "Until now, I've danced pretty much every year. I've danced both in Sandia and San Juan. I danced the Basket Dance and Harvest Dance recently."

Summer is a time for feasting, for travel to the Tekakwitha Conference, and for the family to prepare for Indian Market and to gather in their central booth under the Palace of the Governors' portal on the Santa Fe plaza. And every year, in midsummer, Jerry stops her committee work and everything else in order to paint.

I've exhibited every year at [Indian] Market since 1936, I think it was—I don't remember what year I started. But anyway, I have been at it since. All of us show now—Bob, Gene, and Paul. [*] My house is always so dirty after Market I could plant chile in the living room because of all the dirt that accumulates!

[*] I'm just a down-to-earth person, very traditional. In painting, I just use earth colors. And with music, I enjoy a lot of classical music and the Gregorian chants and Indian music.

At an Indian dance, someone said to me one day, "Why, you're just pure Indian!" "Well," I said, "I hope so!"

AFTERWORD
Revisiting

On the last weekend of April 1994, Santa Fe was at its most capricious: cherry blossoms, with an apple-green mist of new leaves against a sky alternately overcast and intense blue. On Friday, it snowed.

Jerry and Aunt Shine joined us at La Fonda Hotel for breakfast, for one of our final joint revisions of the manuscript. After we caught up with family news, we gave them each copies to correct. We pleaded with them not to edit the transcripts of our recent interviews too heavily, to leave them with the oddities of spoken English.

Later, Jerry drove with us up to the Laboratory of Anthropology, Museum of Indian Arts and Culture. Together, we sat in the archives poring over the recently donated files of Dorothy Dunn's meticulous records from the Studio. Jerry saw, for the first time in sixty-five years, art work she had done in Dunn's first classes. She exclaimed with quiet delight and surprise each time she discovered yet another drawing, invitation, or booklet written in her hand. Dunn had kept much—particularly Jerry's work.

After we exhausted ourselves over the files, we took Jerry home. Between family visits and attending a First Communion at Santo Domingo Pueblo, she completed the tedious process of correcting the latest manuscript—including her syntax and ours.

On Saturday, we visited Etel Kramer. She kindly allowed us to photograph the earth-toned *Basket Dancers* painting that her mother, Dorothy Dunn, bought from Jerry, in 1933. It hangs two miles from where Jerry painted it, over sixty years before. Later, we went to Jerry's. Babba, her unruly German shepherd, greeted us. Jerry looked tired, sitting in her armchair surrounded by chapters yet to edit. She thought she might have to give up driving with Aunt Shine to the San Felipe Corn Dance on Sunday so she could finish.

In the kitchen we reviewed the slides of her paintings. In the course of locating earlier photographs Jeanne had given the family, Jerry happened upon several family albums she had not thought to show us before. More precious artifacts of memory spread across the living room. One album contained a school studio portrait of Jerry in her early twenties. She told us Juan carried it in his wallet all his life.

She also found her notes for talks she had given earlier in the week to her educational heirs at the Indian School during which she exhorted them to "go on to college" and "be what you want to be."

She gave a brief personal history and then spoke about the role of traditional Indian women. The talk transcends conflict and paradox:

> Today the world has become very complicated but we all have a place in today's society. Traditional women are strong. They put up with hard life but they survive. The traditional women of today are no different from women of years ago. They are hard workers raising families. The traditional women of today are more involved in the outside world. They go for higher education and therefore are professionals and have good, respectable positions, whether they are employed on the reservation or in urban cities.
>
> They have learned to communicate, share ideas, serve their communities; they help one another. They respect the elders and respect each other. The traditional women are very caring, understanding and always helping.
>
> The traditional women in today's society also participate in religious activities, whether Indian, Catholic, or other denominations. They are involved in the good things of life—board members in crafts organizations; school boards; and in health, museum, and cul-

tural organizations. They also get involved in athletic activities, museum lectures, and concerts.

The traditional women continue to learn, working on crafts, pottery, weaving, and some are very involved in art, in volunteer work, and still keep families together. Many traditional women share knowledge in the non-Indian world as well as in their communities.

The traditional women help preserve our Indian culture, our traditional language, songs, prayers, and the language. If lost, we have nothing.

APPENDIX
Related Studies

As we worked on the book, two sources provided a wider context in which to understand Jerry's life. Since our recording of Jerry's narrative on her school life, Sally Hyer has published *One House, One Voice, One Heart* (1990), an oral history of the Santa Fe Indian School. Much of what Jerry told us about her school experiences in 1988 she also provided to Hyer. Hyer's broader examination of this school experience has been valuable. Also, Dorothy Dunn [Kramer]'s personal records, recently archived at the Laboratory of Anthropology of the Museum of Indian Arts and Culture, and her book, *American Indian Painting of the Southwest and Plains Areas* (1968), provided essential information from the perspective of the Studio's founder.

After we completed the book, we reviewed related research methodologies documented since we conceptualized and began our work in 1977. It was encouraging to see that others had also been experimenting with alternative ways to better hold the tension between subjective and objective approaches to life narratives. What follows is a brief review of some of the conceptual areas in which their research converges with ours. Of greatest interest to us were Lila Abu-Lughod's *Writing Women's Worlds: Bedouin Stories* (1993), Gretchen M. Bataille and Kathleen Mullen Sands' *American Indian Women: Telling Their Lives* (1984), Mary Catherine Bateson's

Composing a Life (1989), Mary Field Belenky et al.'s *Women's Ways of Knowing* (1986), editors James Clifford and George E. Marcus' *Writing Culture: The Poetics and Politics of Ethnography* (1986), Julie Cruikshank's *Life Lived Like a Story* (1990), Judith V. Jordan et al.'s *Women's Growth in Connection: Writings from the Stone Center* (1991), Francoise Lionnet's *Autobiographical Voices: Race, Gender, Self-Portraiture* (1989), Tsianina Lomawaima's *They Called It Prairie Light* (1994), Trinh T. Minh-ha's *Woman Native Other* (1993), Greg Sarris' *Keeping Slug Woman Alive: A Holistic Approach to American Indian Texts* (1993), and Leonard Shlain's *Art and Physics: Parallel Visions in Space, Time, and Light* (1991).

Many of these researchers believe, as we do, that how a narrative is structured reflects the belief system of the narrator. When a story is told to another, its actual narrative structure reflects not only the belief system of the storyteller but also that of the recorder. Influences on narrative structure are philosophical, cultural, and personal. Minh-ha (1993) and Shlain (1991) mention the strong influence of the worldview of the narrator. Minh-ha observes that we routinely look for the underlying structure in a story as though it were something separable from the content. She severely criticizes this stance:

> It is, once more, as if form and content stand apart; as if the structure can remain fixed, immutable, independent of and unaffected by the changes the narratives undergo; as if a structure can only function as a standard mold within the old determinist schema of cause and product. (1993, 141)

Shlain (1991, 290–304) also observes that the structures of many of our stories, particularly in the genres of autobiography, biography, and the novel, have been strongly connected to our prevailing worldview. He adds that, in the Middle Ages, time, space, and point of view were believed to be flexible and unboundaried, and narratives tended to reflect similar beliefs. Later, deterministic views of the cosmos saw time as linear, space as absolute and measurable, and point of view as fixed and located in a detached observer. These views spawned tales told chronologically from a fixed, invisible, "objective" viewpoint.

Several of these authors mention, too, the frequent use of the hero myth to structure a life. A measurable universe allows us to measure our progress, set goals, follow trajectories, and attain the grail. The hero myth itself reflects certain beliefs about the universe and life; these beliefs are not universally applicable, particularly to many non-Western cultures and to many women in many cultures, including Western. The hero myth has, in fact, underpinned much Western psychological developmental theory until recently. Now it is being questioned as an appropriate template for women's development; in many, if not all, cultures, women's full maturation may have more to do with capacity to establish and sustain connection than with some heroic ideal of separation (Gilligan 1982; Jordan et al. 1991). Jelinek also points out that women do not usually describe their lives as the heroic, uninterrupted pursuit of goals (1980, 17–19). Bateson makes a similar point:

> There is a pattern deeply rooted in myth and folklore that recurs in biography and may create inappropriate expectations and blur our ability to see the actual shape of lives. Much biography of exceptional people is built around the image of a quest . . . toward an end that is specific, even though it is not fully known. . . .
> These assumptions have not been valid for many of history's most creative people, and they are increasingly inappropriate today. (1989, 5–6)

What do these authors see as viable alternatives to the structure of the hero myth with its beginning, middle, end, goal, and linear progression? Jordan et al. (1991) and Bateson (1989) suggest that lives that appear diffuse are also worthy of study. As Bateson suggests,

> These are not lives without commitment, but rather lives in which commitments are continually refocused and redefined. (1989, 9)
> Once you begin to see these lives of multiple commitments and multiple beginnings as an emerging pattern rather than an aberration, it takes no more than a second look to discover the models for that reinvention on every side, to look for the followers of visions that are not fixed but that evolve from day to day. (1989, 17)

Minh-ha also draws attention to this alternative when she rejects viewing life as a classical Western drama structured by a beginning, development, climax, and dénouement:

> Sometimes it just drifts along; it may go on year after year without development, without climax, without definite beginnings or endings. Or it may accumulate climax upon climax, and if one chooses to mark it with beginnings and endings, then everything has a beginning and an ending. (1993, 143)

Cultural considerations are further raised by Minh-ha (1993) and Abu-Lughod (1993). They point out that, despite the work of groundbreakers such as Gilligan (1983), nothing universal can be inferred reliably about all women or about all women's lives. Each culture influences its women's lives, creating different forms. Bataille and Sands discuss the inappropriateness of fitting American Indian women's stories into conventional Western autobiographical structures. "Creative imagination, invention in adaptation, and flexibility in form have been accepted as essential characteristics of poetry and fiction, but the respectability and existence of these qualities are controversial in autobiography" (1984, 15). They further assert that the very content of these women's stories contradicts the conventional selection of material for classical Western autobiography, which emphasizes individual achievement (e.g., the hero myth). Rather, indigenous women's autobiographies share certain basic characteristics with oral forms:

> emphasis on event, attention to the sacredness of language, concern with landscape, affirmation of cultural values and tribal solidarity. These properties of the oral tradition derive from a concern for communal welfare, the subordination of the individual to the collective needs of the tribe. (3–4)
> . . . Female Indian autobiographies . . . concentrate on everyday events and activities and family crisis events—birth, naming, puberty, marriage, and motherhood. (8)

They also observe that American Indian women tell their life stories in words conservative in emotional connotation. Even moments of crisis are likely to be described without much intensity of language. Such understatement is not an indication of repression or absence of emotional states but often evidence that the narrator simply takes that state for granted. (17)

With regard to actual structure, Bataille and Sands (1984) share the opinion that:

> There is a sense in most Indian women's autobiographies of the connectedness of all things, of personal life flow, and episodes often are not sequential but linked thematically to establish a pattern of character developing through the response to private experience. (8)

Each of these authors also underscores the critical importance of the relationship between storyteller and recorder and the difficulties of a biculturally composed narrative. However, they disagree about how and whether to alter the inherent structure of the narrative: Bataille and Sands favor a thematic approach; Minh-ha, Sarris, and Abu-Lughod value minimal intervention. Bataille and Sands, for example, observe that the connection between events is assumed by the narrator, who understands her own culture and her communal orientation and so, as mediator between worlds, "the editor structures the oral narrative from the essential themes, aspects of character, point of view, and experiences of the narrator" (14). Sarris, however, is critical of this thematic approach:

> [Bataille and Sands] seem to forget that these themes or thematic patterns not only may have been invented by them for the texts and understood in terms of their particular interests (and their lives as non-Indian women), but also may emerge in the written documents as a result of the particular interests of the recorder-editors. Bataille and Sands never question how their themes may or may not be relevant from the point of view of the Indian women narrators. (1993, 89–90)

Sarris further laments the unconscious ways in which editor-recorders alter subtle meaning and form by changing grammar to make it "better" English and sequence to make it more readable. He demonstrates how deleting a repeated word can alter meaning and significance given to a person, event, place, or thing. (The dilemma is heightened when, as in our case, the storyteller instructs the editor-recorders to edit transcripts and rewrite bicultural informal oral style to read more like formal written Western style.)

Abu-Lughod (1993) adds to our understanding of the complexity of the narrator-editor's task; she reminds us of the extensive work done by feminist theorists in many fields to expose the hidden power dynamics operative in many situations. She also voices concerns about the indirect exercise of power in researcher generalizations, attempts at objectivity, and subsequent homogenization. Both Abu-Lughod (1993) and Cruikshank (1990) articulate as fully as they can what academic precedents they are trying to either overcome or work within while also intentionally respecting their own personal subjectivity. However, even Abu-Lughod acknowledges she needed to find a compromise that had integrity yet felt risky with regard to both her structuring of the Bedouin women's stories and her own ethnographic stance:

> I selected the stories and wove them into a pattern on the basis of conjunction between Bedouin women's interest in and attention to certain issues and the salience of these issues for specific audiences in the West. (16)
>
> The arrangement of the stories into chapters follows an anthropological logic. (18)
>
> . . . In short, I have sought a presence somewhere between the extremes of total erasure of the ethnographer's self . . . and imposition of his or her presence as an equal participant. (29)

Jacquelyn Dowd Hall also comments on the necessity for some conscious viewpoint:

> We have challenged the illusion of objectivity and given up the arrogance of believing that we can, once and for all, get our foremothers right. . . . Only by telling new stories and telling our

stories anew can we glimpse the truths that emerge not once and for all but all in their own good time. (Alpern et al., eds., 1992, 11)

Sharon O'Brien, author of *Willa Cather: The Emerging Voice* (1986) describes her struggle with similar forces and decisions ("My Willa Cather: How Writing Her Story Shaped My Own," *New York Times Book Review*, February 20, 1994, 25.) She is only too aware that "cultural and narrative structures shape our approach to biography whether we know it or not." She describes her rejection of chronology and linearity in writing the biography, believing herself to be creating a new biographical form. Only later did she realize she had been unconsciously influenced by a vision of a feminist bildungsroman, a vision of emergence.

Sarris (1993) offers a hope for embracing these impossible challenges. He reiterates Stephen Tyler's simple suggestion that all aspects of the narrator and editor-recorder relationship be clarified:

Tyler and many other contemporary social scientists . . . stress the importance of polyvocality in the written document, the presence of multiple voices. They call for reflexivity, asking ethnographers to account for their conclusions, for their notions of truth and knowledge, and for the political and historical consequences of their work. They argue that for crosscultural communication to be open and effective, interlocutors must be aware of their boundaries, both personal and cultural, so that they might know the limits on and possibilities for understanding one another in the exchange. That is, in understanding another person and culture you must simultaneously understand yourself. The process is ongoing, an endeavor aimed not at a final transparent understanding of the Other or of the self, but at continued communication, at an ever-widening understanding of both. (1993, 5–6)

It is just such a process that Jordan et al. (1991) suggest is the true goal of conscious mutual relationships. And it is within just such a process of continued communication, in the midst of our continually widening understanding of Jerry Montoya and ourselves, that we leave this narrative.

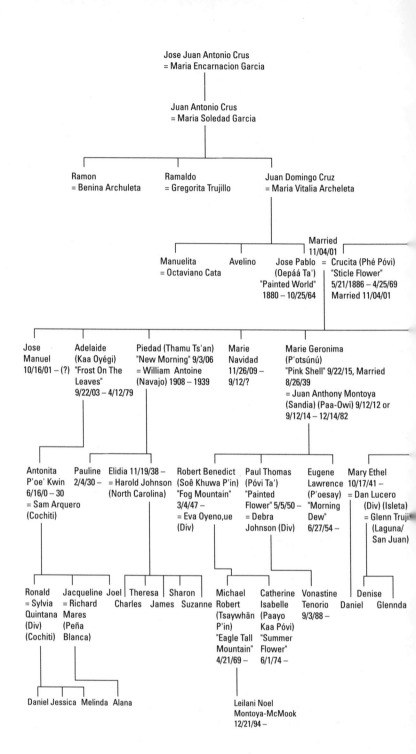

Jose Juan Antonio Crus
= Maria Encarnacion Garcia

Juan Antonio Crus
= Maria Soledad Garcia

Ramon
= Benina Archuleta

Ramaldo
= Gregorita Trujillo

Juan Domingo Cruz
= Maria Vitalia Archeleta

Manuelita
= Octaviano Cata

Avelino

Jose Pablo
(Oepáá Ta')
"Painted World"
1880 – 10/25/64

Married
11/04/01
= Crucita (Phé Póvi)
"Sticle Flower"
5/21/1886 – 4/25/69
Married 11/04/01

Jose
Manuel
10/16/01 – (?)

Adelaide
(Kaa Oyégi)
"Frost On The
Leaves"
9/22/03 – 4/12/79

Piedad (Thamu Ts'an)
"New Morning" 9/3/06
= William Antoine
(Navajo) 1908 – 1939

Marie
Navidad
11/26/09 –
9/12/?

Marie Geronima
(P'otsúnú)
"Pink Shell" 9/22/15, Married
8/26/39
= Juan Anthony Montoya
(Sandia) (Paa-Owi) 9/12/12 or
9/12/14 – 12/14/82

Antonita
P'oe' Kwin
6/16/0 – 30
= Sam Arquero
(Cochiti)

Pauline
2/4/30 –

Elidia 11/19/38 –
= Harold Johnson
(North Carolina)

Robert Benedict
(Soê Khuwa P'in)
"Fog Mountain"
3/4/47 –
= Eva Oyeno,ue
(Div)

Paul Thomas
(Póvi Ta')
"Painted
Flower" 5/5/50 –
= Debra
Johnson (Div)

Eugene
Lawrence
(P'oesay)
"Morning
Dew"
6/27/54 –

Mary Ethel
10/17/41 –
= Dan Lucero
(Div) (Isleta)
= Glenn Truji
(Laguna/
San Juan)

Ronald
= Sylvia
Quintana
(Div)
(Cochiti)

Jacqueline
= Richard
Mares
(Peña
Blanca)

Joel

Theresa
Charles

Sharon
James

Suzanne

Michael
Robert
(Tsaywhän
P'in)
"Eagle Tall
Mountain"
4/21/69 –

Catherine
Isabelle
(Paayo
Kaa Póvi)
"Summer
Flower"
6/1/74 –

Vonastine
Tenorio
9/3/88 –

Denise

Daniel   Glennda

Daniel Jessica Melinda Alana

Leilani Noel
Montoya-McMook
12/21/94 –

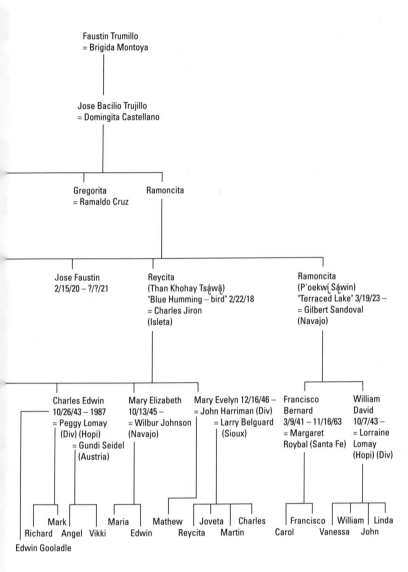

Faustin Trumillo
= Brigida Montoya

Jose Bacilio Trujillo
= Domingita Castellano

Gregorita   Ramoncita
= Ramaldo Cruz

Jose Faustin   Reycita   Ramoncita
2/15/20 – ?/?/21   (Than Khohay Tsậwậ)   (P'oekwí Sậwin)
                      "Blue Humming – bird" 2/22/18   "Terraced Lake" 3/19/23 –
                      = Charles Jiron   = Gilbert Sandoval
                      (Isleta)   (Navajo)

Charles Edwin   Mary Elizabeth   Mary Evelyn 12/16/46 –   Francisco   William
10/26/43 – 1987   10/13/45 –   = John Harriman (Div)   Bernard   David
= Peggy Lomay   = Wilbur Johnson   = Larry Belguard   3/9/41 – 11/16/63 10/7/43 –
(Div) (Hopi)   (Navajo)   (Sioux)   = Margaret   = Lorraine
= Gundi Seidel   Roybal (Santa Fe) Lomay
(Austria)   (Hopi) (Div)

      Mark   Maria   Mathew   Joveta   Charles   Francisco William Linda
Richard   Angel Vikki   Edwin   Reycita   Martin   Carol   Vanessa John
Edwin Gooladle

REFERENCES

Abu-Lughod, Lila. *Writing Women's Worlds: Bedouin Stories*. Berkeley: University of California Press, 1993.

Alpern, Sara, et al. *The Challenge of Feminist Biography: Writing the Lives of Modern American Women*, Urbana: University of Illinois Press, 1992.

"Annual Exhibition of the Indian School." *El Palacio*, 1945, vol. 52, no. 5, 81–82.

"Annual Indian School Exhibit." *El Palacio*, May 1944, vol. 51, no. 5, 83–84.

"At the Art Gallery." *El Palacio*, June 1948, vol. 55, no. 6, 185.

Bataille, Gretchen M., and Kathleen Mullen Sands. *American Indian Women: Telling Their Lives*. Lincoln and London: University of Nebraska Press, 1984.

Bateson, Mary Catherine. *Composing a Life*. New York: A Plume Book, 1989.

Belenky, Mary Field, et al. *Women's Ways of Knowing*. New York: Basic Books, 1986.

Boss, Suzanne K. Untitled article. *Southwest Association on Indian Affairs Quarterly*, Winter 1966, vol. 3, no. 4.

Clifford, James, and George E. Marcus, eds. *Writing Culture: The Poetics and Politics of Ethnography*. Berkeley: University of California Press, 1986.

Cruikshank, Julie. *Life Lived Like a Story*. Lincoln and London: University of Nebraska Press, 1990.

93 DDK. See Kramer, Dorothy Dunn.

Dunn, Dorothy. *American Indian Painting of the Southwest and Plains Areas*. Albuquerque: University of New Mexico Press, 1968.

———. "American Indian Painting." *Civil Service Arts Quarterly*, London, 1936.

———. "Young Indians Revive Their Native Arts." *School Arts*, November 1936.

Dutton, Bertha P. *New Mexico Indians and the Arizona Neighbors*. Santa Fe: New Mexico Association on Indian Affairs, 1955.

Ewing, Robert A. "The New Indian Art." *El Palacio*, Spring 1969, vol. 76, no. 1, 33–39.

Fisher, Reginald, ed. and comp. *An Art Directory of New Mexico*. Albuquerque: School of American Research with University of New Mexico Press, 1947.

Gilligan, Carol. *In a Different Voice: Psychological Theory and Women's Development*. Cambridge: Harvard University Press, 1982.

Hall, Jacquelyn Dowd. "Introduction." In Sara Alpern, Joyce Antler, Elisabeth Israel Perry, and Ingrid Winther Scobie, eds., *The Challenge of Feminist Biography: Writing the Lives of Modern American Women*. Urbana: University of Illinois Press, 1992.

Highwater, Jamake. "Controversy in Native American Art." In Edwin L. Wade, ed., *The Arts of the North American Indian: Native Traditions in Evolution*. New York: Philbrook Art Center and Hudson Hills Press, 1986.

Hoffman, Gerhard. "Frames of Reference: Native American Art in the Context of Modern and Postmodern Art." In Edwin L. Wade, ed., *The Arts of the North American Indian: Native Traditions in Evolution*. New York: Philbrook Art Center and Hudson Hills Press, 1986.

Hyer, Sally. *One House, One Voice, One Heart: Native American Education at the Santa Fe Indian School*. Santa Fe: Museum of New Mexico Press, 1990.

Jacobson, Oscar Brousse, and Jeanne D'Ucel. *Les Peintres Indiens d'Amerique (American Indian Painters)*. Nice, France: Editions d'Art, Szwedzicki, 1950.

Jelinek, Estelle C., ed. *Women's Autobiography: Essays in Criticism*. Bloomington: Indiana University Press, 1980.

Jordan, Judith V., et al. *Women's Growth in Connection: Writings from the Stone Center*. New York: The Guilford Press, 1991.

Kramer, Dorothy Dunn. "Dorothy Dunn Kramer Papers," Archives of the Laboratory of Anthropology, Museum of Indian Arts and Culture. Abbreviated as 93 DDK in the text.

Kurath, Gertrude Prokosch, with Antonio García. *Music and Dance of the Tewa Pueblos*. Santa Fe: Museum of New Mexico, 1970.

Lionnet, Francoise. *Autobiographical Voices: Race, Gender, Self-Portraiture*. Ithaca and London: Cornell University Press, 1989.

Lomawaima, Tsianina. *They Called It Prairie Light*. Lincoln and London: University of Nebraska Press, 1994.

Minh-ha, Trinh T. *Woman Native Other*. Bloomington: Indiana University Press, 1993.

Morang, Alfred. *El Palacio*, 1940, vol. 47, no. 5, 117–118.

"Mrs. Montoya Exhibits Art at Library." *New Mexican*, Los Alamos edition, July 27, 1967.

O'Brien, Sharon. "My Willa Cather: How Writing Her Story Shaped My Own." *New York Times Book Review*, February 20, 1994.

Ortiz, Alfonso. *The Tewa World: Space, Time, Being, and Becoming in a Pueblo Society*. Chicago and London: The University of Chicago Press, 1969.

"Pueblo Painter Po-tsunu Exhibits." *Santa Fe Scene*, August 15, 1959, 22.

Rehnstrand, J. "Young Indians Revive Their Native Arts." *School Arts*, Nov. 1936, 137–138.

"Review of American Indian Art Exhibit." *New Mexican*, Sunday, November 11, 1962.

Rush, Olive. "Exhibit of Indian Paintings." *El Palacio*, 1934, vol. 36, nos. 20–26, 200.

———. "Annual Indian Art Show." *El Palacio*, 1937, vol. 42, nos. 19–21, 105–108.

Sarris, Greg. *Keeping Slug Woman Alive: A Holistic Approach to American Indian Texts*. Berkeley: University of California Press, 1993.

Shlain, Leonard. *Art and Physics: Parallel Visions in Space, Time, and Light*. New York: William Morrow and Company, 1991.

"Show By Po-tsunu To Open Sunday." *Albuquerque Journal*, March 4, 1965.

Snodgrass, Jeanne O. *American Indian Painters: A Biographical Directory*.

New York: Museum of the American Indian, Heye Foundation, 1968.

Sturtevant, William C. "The Meanings of Native American Art." In Edwin L. Wade, ed., *The Arts of the North American Indian: Native Traditions in Evolution*. New York: Philbrook Art Center and Hudson Hills Press, 1986.

Téwa Khawa: Téwa Names. Santa Ana: Summer Institute of Linguistics, 1970.

Wade, Edwin L. "Straddling the Cultural Fence: The Conflict for Ethnic Artists within Pueblo Societies." In Wade, ed., *The Arts of the North American Indian: Native Traditions in Evolution*. New York: Philbrook Art Center and Hudson Hills Press, 1986.

Warner, John Anson. "The Individual in Native American Art: A Sociological View." In Edwin L. Wade, ed., *The Arts of the North American Indian: Native Traditions in Evolution*. New York: Philbrook Art Center and Hudson Hills Press, 1986.

Who's Who in American Art. New York: R. R. Bowker, 1962.

Who's Who in New Mexico. Albuquerque: The Abousleman Company, 1946.

Who's Who in the West. Chicago: Marquis, 1965–1966, vol. 9, 553.

INDEX

individualism," 182. *See also* Traditional versus modern art debate

Education, Indian: abuses, 35; mission schools, 37. *See also* Boarding schools, federal

Eight Northern Pueblos, 159, 160, 171, 208, 214

Elidia Antoine Johnson (Piedad's daughter), 86; communal feasts, 150; exhibits, 200; home, 15, 135

Embroidery, 61

Ewing, Robert A., 122–24

Exhibits: Amerika Haus (Germany), 195; Brooklyn Museum, 192; Chicago, 192; de Young Museum (San Francisco), 192; Detroit, 192; family exhibit at Palo Alto, California, 200; Fred Wilson's, 99; German American Institute (Germany), 195; Governor's Gallery, 211; Hall of Ethnology (Santa Fe), 193; invitations, 177; Knoxville, Tennessee, 99; Legend's Cafe, 211; Mesa Public Library, 199; Mesa Public Library (Los Alamos), 212; Museum of the American Indian, 198; Museum of Fine Arts at Stanford University, 71; Museum of Fine Arts (Santa Fe), 195; Museum of New Mexico, 99, 129, 192–93, 193; Museum of New Mexico annual May show, 64, 65, 69–70, 101–3, 191; Museum of New Mexico Gallery, 126; Nacogdoches, Texas, 99; Oke Oweenge Crafts Cooperative, 200; Philbrook Art Center, 196; Phoenix, 211; San Francisco Gold Gate Exposition (1939), 80, 191; Santa Fe Indian Market, 176–77; Scottsdale Arts and Crafts Center, 195; Second National Exhibition of American Art (Rockefeller Center), 71; Second Scottsdale Annual Painting Exhibition, 195; Smith College Club, 126–27; spring exhibits for San Juan artists, 164; Symbol Gallery of Arts (Albuquerque), 195; Tenth Annual Festival of American Folklife (Washington, D.C.), 199–200; Valley National Bank of Española, 198; Yonemoto's Fine Arts Gallery, 196–98

Family life: ceremonials and, 139; Pueblo stories and, 4

Faris, Chester, 38; appreciation of Pueblo culture, 144; discipline, 43; as Jerry's teacher, 157; leaves SFIS, 67; multiculturalism, 53; reforms, 50; security for students, 46–47; supports painting studio, 58; trip with students, 46–48; visits Santa Fe Indian School, 100

Farming: arts and crafts with, 54; by Pablo Cruz, 17, 19

140–43; in Robert Montoya's
art, 184; for white people, 141
Nature motifs, Jerry explains,
78–79, 180, 201
Navajo crafts, 172; Reservation,
46, 56; students, 92
New, Lloyd Kiva: antipathy for
Dunn and Studio style,
123–24; at adult education
workshop, 172; director of
Institute for American Indian
Arts (IAIA), 1967–1980, 129;
first contact with Dunn,
75–76; Jerry at summer classes
with, 127–28; opponent of
Studio, 92
New Mexico Commission on the
Status of Women, 214
New Mexico State Department of
Education, 132
Northern Arts and Crafts
Commission, 214
Northern Pueblos Agency (BIA),
157, 168

Ojo Caliente, 20
Oke Oweenege Crafts
Cooperative: architecture, 13,
167; booth at Santa Fe Indian
Market, 188; building to
house, 166–67, 170; competi-
tion, 171; development,
172–73; established in San
Juan Day School, 36, 165–68;
exhibits at, 200; invited to
Washington, D.C., 199–200;
Jerry's contribution, 170–71

Oral history, 9, 28, 228
Oregon College of Education,
140, 161–62, 168, 172
Orem, Virginia E., 133–35
Original action and traditional
values, 85
Originality issue, 62, 63
Ortiz, Alfonso, viii, 165, 199–200
Oyenque, Eva, 163, 170, 209, 210

Painting: Jerry's paintings,
177–78, 180; miniature, 114;
reasons for, 8; tribal traditions,
53, 175
Palmer, Ignatius, 95
Pauline Antoine (Piedad's daughter), 86; communal feasts, 150;
home, 15; illness, 208
Philbrook Art Center, 125
Phoenix Indian School, 75–76;
praised, 90
Photography by Jeanne Shutes, 9,
10
Piedad Cruz Antoine: cares for
Jerry, 20; as child, 18; communal feasts, 150; education, 35,
41; exhibits, 200; as godparent,
105; home, 15; illness, 208;
Jerry's wedding, 86; pottery, 25;
resemblance to Crucita, 27;
retirement, 208; sewing, 23;
translation of New Testament
into Téwa, 160; washing
clothes, 24; works at Indian
Hospital, 87
Pojoaque Pueblo, 215
Political militancy of 1960s, 122

175; function and, 186, 188; Jerry's commitment to, 83–85, 176, 177, 178, 193, 198; traditional dress, 23–24, 153

Traditional versus modern art debate, 203–4; changes of 1960s, 122–25; combination praised, 103; heritage of tribal traditions, 81, 94–95; Jerry's consistency and, 9, 176; Lloyd New and, 127–28; Plains ledger drawings, 122; use of non-traditional materials, 64

"Traditional woman," Jerry's concept of, 84–85, 222–23

Transcripts, editing principles, 7

Travel: Atlanta, 45–49; Claremont, California, 110–11; National Folk Festival (St. Louis), 98; New York with student winner of American Magazine Youth Forum Contest, 95; proposed trip to Europe, 133–35; Smithsonian Institute, 206; Washington, D.C., 47

Tribal identity and schools, 38

Tribal traditions in American Indian art, 81, 175

Trujillo, Ascension, 80

Tsebetsaye, Roger, 80, 194, 195

Trujillo, Crucita. *See* Crucita Trujillo Cruz

Tsireh, Awa, 79

Tskiumu P'in, 141, 142, 150

Uniformity, ethic of, 178

United Pueblos Agency (BIA), 26, 129, 132

Values: as conservative, 83–85; consistency of Jerry's, 7; from parents, 30, 31–32

Velarde, Pablita, 79, 116

Vigil, Martín, 46

Virgin Mary, 153

Vocational education, 98

War Captain, 195

Water, fetching, 32–33

Weaving, 61; by cacique, 28

What My Community Contributes to the Nation, 95–97

Wheelwright, Mary, 102

Wheelwright Museum (Santa Fe), 214

Women, food at ceremonials, 140

Work ethic, 5, 44

World War, II, 100–101

Worlds, as organizational concept, 8, 139

Yazz, Beatien, 79, 81

Zia Pueblo, 46, 144

Under the Portal, 203